LOVE AND STRUGGLE IN MAO'S THOUGHT

ORBIS BOOKS
Maryknoll, New York 10545

Love and Struggle in Mao's Thought

Raymond L. Whitehead

Copyright © 1977 by Orbis Books

Orbis Books, Maryknoll, New York 10545

Printed in the United States of America

Library of Congress Cataloging in Publication Data

Whitehead, Raymond L
  Love and struggle in Mao's thought.

  Includes bibliographical references.
  1. Mao, Tse-tung, 1893-   —Philosophy. 2. China
—Politics and government—1949-   I. Title.
DS778.M3W49   171   76-41902
ISBN 0-88344-289-2
ISBN 0-88344-290-6 pbk.

To the real heroines and heroes—
those whose work and sweat,
suffering and death,
love and struggle,
move life, thought, and history forward.

"The masses are the real heroes, while we ourselves are often childish and ignorant; without this understanding it is impossible to acquire even the most rudimentary knowledge."

—MAO ZEDONG

CONTENTS

PREFACE

A word of explanation about style may be useful to the reader. The system of romanized spelling for Chinese words here generally follows that which has been adopted in the People's Republic of China. This system is gaining international acceptance and will likely replace other systems now in use. I have used this system almost totally (Mao Zedong instead of Mao Tse-tung, for example). In the notes, and when quoting, I retain the spelling used in the original source. Also proper nouns are given the older romanization where use of the new system could cause confusion. (For example, I retain the traditional spellings of Peking, Hong Kong, Chiang Kai-shek, and Sun Yat-sen.) The reader may wish to refer to the glossary of Chinese names and terms at the end of the book.

I have tried to avoid sexist language and the use of masculine pronouns when both male and female are indicated, although in some instances this seemed unavoidable. It should be noted that in Chinese, terms such as hero, mankind, and chairman do not use masculine or feminine forms, a distinction which appears in the English translation.

I use the terms "Maoism" and "Maoist" even though these are not current in China. "Marxism-Leninism-Mao Zedong Thought" is too cumbersome in English. I use "Maoism" simply as a shortened form of that Chinese expression. "Maoist" is used only to mean a Chinese follower of Marxism-Leninism-Mao Zedong Thought.

A special word of appreciation must be given to those who helped in various ways to prepare this book. Rhea M.

Whitehead's contributions were invaluable in developing the basic analysis of this study. Luella Kam gave great assistance on the Chinese terminology and the background of Mao's philosophy. The editorial work of Tom Fenton and Mary Heffron improved the manuscript significantly. DeWitt Barnett read the entire manuscript and offered many useful suggestions. Several versions of the manuscript were patiently and faithfully typed by Christina Lai. My thanks to all these friends and many others in Hong Kong and elsewhere who helped me along the way.

In developing the ethical framework for this study, I benefited at an earlier stage from the critical guidance of Professors John Bennett, Roger Shinn, Searle Bates, and the late Johannes Hoekendijk. A comparison of Mao's ethic with that of the Western Christian tradition, a task in which I was then engaged, remains on the agenda for a future book.

INTRODUCTION

This book is about the ethical thought of Mao Zedong (Mao Tse-tung). In Maoist writings ethical concern is expressed in terms of the question, "Whom do I serve?" In Maoist theory one is always confronted with a decision either to serve the people or to serve one's own selfish interests. The common way of posing ethical questions in the West is in terms of what is good, what is a good society, or what is right action and behavior. Formulating the problem as "Whom do I serve?" is not in conflict with these Western formulations. Putting it the Maoist way, however, immediately makes the ethical issue concrete and personal. One is not dealing with an abstract problem of the nature of the good, but with the down-to-earth question of how one's lifestyle and action relate to the people.

Mao's ethic, as the title of this book implies, is an ethic both of love and struggle.

Love for the people is integral to Mao's vision, although the term "love" is not used by Maoists as often or as facilely as by Western ethicists. In China the term "unity" is preferred. "Unity" carries some of the meanings of love, such as the reunion of hostile factions (a popular motto is "unity-struggle-unity"). Combined with the call to serve the people, "unity" can also mean love in a dynamic sense.

Our understanding of Mao's ethic would be distorted, however, if the themes of love and unity in his thought led us to neglect the central importance of struggle. Society, according to Mao, is marked by continual class struggle; this social struggle is reflected in each individual's thought. Struggle does move toward the final goal of love and unity—the classless society—but Mao's revolutionary ethic does not take this final goal of history as a present reality. Although Maoism envisions a classless society at the end of history, this does not mean that Maoism is a Western-type ethic that extols love and reconciliation yet overlooks the need for class struggle. I will attempt to show why the emphasis on social struggle and thought struggle gives a dynamic and creative impulse to Mao's ethic and why this ethic is significant for us.

My treatment of Mao's ethic is frankly a sympathetic one, although I am not a Maoist. I belong to the "dominant" American minority group called WASPs, white Anglo-Saxon Protestants. By education I am a middle-class liberal. I could claim a proletarian heritage since my parents were unskilled workers. If I were running for political office in America, where it is a virtue not to be but to have been poor, I could get some mileage from my background. An honest position here is that I am an average American who has been impressed by Mao's ethic, and who writes from that viewpoint.

On occasion I have been called a Maoist, in derision. My response is *bugandang* ("I would not dare accept the honor"). I have done nothing to deserve the appellation. If by the term "Maoist" is meant one who has studied Mao's writings and been influenced by his thought, then it is applicable to me. This would be in the sense that another might be a Kantian or Aristotelian in philosophical orientation.

I realize that it is not easy for the average American to come to a positive appreciation of Mao's ethic. It is necessary for us to overcome certain traditional prejudices, such as the fear of the "yellow peril" and the assumption of white Western superiority. In addition there is the relatively new fear of the "red menace," which sees Chinese Communists as a threat to our security. This was exemplified in Dean Rusk's nightmare of hundreds of millions of Chinese Communists armed with nuclear weapons. There is another prejudice among those who seem to feel the Chinese Communists can do no wrong and that all we have to do is copy the Chinese experience. The Chinese are human beings struggling with human problems.

In explaining my appreciation of the progress they have made and what I think we can learn from them, it may sound as though I fall into the second kind of prejudice. In overcoming the more prevalent negative images I may put too much emphasis on the positive, but my intention is to arrive at a clear and balanced judgment.

There have been several developments in recent years that make it easier for Americans to understand the Chinese experience. One of these has been the official détente between Peking and Washington, paving the way for exchange visits and a freer flow of information. This has meant a demystification of China, making it possible to look at that society more realistically.

More importantly, there has been a changing consciousness in America as our society has gone through a series of social movements. These have included the women's liberation movement, the antiwar movement, the black revolution, the native American movement, the rising consciousness of Chicanos—especially the United Farm Workers—and a whole range of movements among other ethnic groups. Although these changes may have caused some people to try to turn the clock back in a nostalgic effort to recover "the good old days," for others it has resulted in an openness to a new way of viewing the world. If we have had our arrogance about the American way shaken, we may be more willing to look at alternative societies, including China.

Internationally, the developments in Indochina have shown, for those who are willing to learn, that the unbridled use of American military power may be neither beneficent nor effective. More Americans are willing to recognize the imperial dimension of our foreign policy and are led to seek a new way of relating to the world which is neither militaristic nor isolationist.

We have also witnessed the damaging effects of an economic and social system which destroys the environment, extracts resources from Third World countries while leaving their people in desperate poverty, and tolerates millions of poor and jobless in the world's richest nation.

In pointing out these developments I am not denigrating America. As we move into the third century since the American revolution it is necessary, it seems to me, to do some stock-taking on how our revolution was able to exclude so many groups from equal rights and foster a plundering attitude towards the world's resources.

A new American patriotism is necessary, one that can appreciate the advances made in the United States and still see the tasks left undone. This new patriotism will have to be built upon a vision of what the U.S.A. can be. It will affirm the struggles of workers, Indians, slaves, Slavs, women, and others as part of what the nation is all about. It will also mean a vision of a nation without economic exploitation domestically or internationally, and one in which the natural environment is preserved for the benefit of all.

It will be a difficult struggle to achieve such a vision. I do not know what strategy or tactics will be used. I do not know what bitterness or suffering may be encountered. I do not know how long it will take. But given the pain and heartache and indignity and injustice that many of our present policies entail, there is no choice but to seek some alternative. The new America envisioned will be an enriching one for all of us, except those who want to live well at the expense of other people's misery.

Mao's ethic and the Chinese experience will not provide us with answers to our problems. I am not suggesting that we follow the Chinese way. The Chinese experience is one among many. We should also seek to learn from those who have struggled in our own country and in other countries to overcome the forces of racism, sexism, and exploitation in all forms. In finding American answers to American problems, however, there are aspects of the Chinese revolutionary ethic that are worthy of our consideration.

As an American I have found the study of Mao's ethic helpful because of its realistic approach to the question of struggle. The American context, as I have described it, is one with many built-in conflicts. A tendency of people concerned about ethics is to look for ways to avoid, reduce, or resolve conflicts. What Mao's ethic suggests is that the way to unity is through struggle. A premature attempt to find reconciliation without struggle may only function to preserve an unjust status quo.

From the perspective of the struggle ethic, all other issues, such as justice, reconciliation, equal rights, social harmony, and personal happiness, are seen in terms of the exploitative or the nonexploitative use of power. Power has political, economic, and social dimensions. For example, in American society justice and equal rights are seen as legal or political issues. The Maoist ethic would require a critique of the way in which vast differences in wealth or social position lead to an unequal application of legal equality. The comparatively light sentences for Watergate criminals compared with long years in crowded jails for the "less advantaged" criminal would be a case in point.

On a nonlegal issue such as reconciliation, the struggle ethic also raises the question of power. If one race or class has vastly superior wealth and prestige in comparison with another race or class, then to seek reconciliation would be fruitless. Until members of the groups can meet each other on a fairly equal basis of power and dignity there is no hope of building genuine unity. This again is relevant to the American situation, where sometimes we seek intergroup "understanding" instead of a needed realignment of power relations.

Another relevant aspect of the struggle ethic is that it ties together all struggles against exploitative power. Mao's ethic developed in the sweep of a revolution in the world's most populous country, which touched all areas of economic, social, political, and cultural life. In the American situation the struggles for justice of various groups have tended to be piecemeal. The Maoist view is that racism and male chauvinism derive from class exploitation. While some may not agree with the Chinese position of seeing the origin of all exploitation in class oppression, the concept of a unified struggle makes sense.

The struggle ethic is also relevant to the American situation because, while taking power seriously, it does not lose sight of its goal. Struggle is not glorified in itself but is seen as a necessary tool for advancing toward the vision of a new society. In Mao's words:

> Of all things in the world, people are the most precious. Under the leadership of the Communist Party, as long as there are people, every kind of miracle can be performed. . . . We believe that revolution can change everything, and that before long there will arise a new China with a big population and a great wealth of products, where life will be abundant and culture will flourish.[1]

In the struggle there is a concern for the well-being of the people. "All people in the revolutionary ranks must care for each other, must love and help each other."[2] The American vision for the future may be expressed in different terms, but the struggle should be motivated by a desire to improve the well-being of all the people.

There are certain objections to the idea of taking the Chinese revolution seriously in our concern for American problems. One of these is that since China is basically an agricultural society with a much different level of development there is little in its experience that is meaningful for Americans. Such an objection is often voiced by the same Americans who would not hesitate to take American solutions—technical, military, aid-oriented, or religious—to rural and "backward" countries at a vastly different level of development. To some extent this objection is part of the American arrogance which says we cannot learn from other, different, societies. Chinese forms may not be directly applicable to other societies, but the Chinese experience is still useful in developing our own solutions to our own problems.

Another objection is that Mao's ethic has not been beneficial for all the people, that many fled, or are unhappy, and still try to flee to Hong Kong. While no statistical evidence is available to say how many Chinese are happy (how many Americans are happy?), it is evident that dissatisfaction continues in China. Mao's ethic is neither perfect in its formulation nor in its application, but it has been relatively successful in revitalizing Chinese society, as I will try to show.

A last objection is that Mao's ethic uses means that we would not condone, such as hatred, violence, brainwashing, and thought control. Many of these charges are Cold War exaggerations. Others stem from the early years of transition when the future was uncertain for the new regime and conflicts were harsh. I will also indicate that enmity and violence have specific functions in Mao's ethic and do not necessarily lead to inhumane results. Final conclusive evidence is not available on some of these questions, and opinions will differ on how to interpret them. Even granting a degree of cruelty in the revolutionary process, I do not feel these aspects negate the creative dimensions of Mao's ethic.

This book grew out of my encounter with Mao's world view and ethic. It began some years ago, first with curiosity and scepticism, and gradually moved to a greater appreciation and understanding. My sources of information are those generally available—the Chinese press and various accounts by other observers. These are augmented by conversations with friends in Hong Kong (of various persuasions) and by a five-week visit to China. The subject is vast, the information conflicting, and my own reflection is still in process. In dealing with Mao's world view I feel I am involved with ideas of immense vitality. Mao's thought is more than a philosophy; it sums up a revolutionary dynamic that has touched the lives of hundreds of millions of people in China and beyond.

In the first chapter I will look at the background in which Mao's philosophy of struggle developed, a time of upheaval, disunity, and suffering. In this period of chaos the Communist revolution represented a movement for the revitalization of Chinese society, but struggle continued even after the victory of the revolution. Three dimensions of Mao's thought which are significant for this study will be discussed. These are his theory of contradiction, his passion for justice, and his vision of human destiny.

In the following two chapters I will describe the way the struggle ethic works out in the new China, first in terms of social conflict, then in terms of personal transformation. This will be followed by a description of lifestyle in revolutionary China, where those who participate in the struggle are called to live simple and frugal lives and to identify with ordinary peasants and workers.

In the fifth chapter I will describe the rejection by Maoists of liberalism and ideas such as humanism, the liberal theory of human nature, and "liberty, equality, and fraternity." Here I will attempt to show why many of the values we hold dear are challenged by Mao's struggle ethic, but yet are reaffirmed in a transformed way in his "revolutionary humanism."

I have been helped and challenged by the study of Mao's ethic. It has led me to formulate more clearly the ethical questions of whom I serve, where I stand, and what is the meaning of conflict and struggle. I am convinced that here we are dealing not simply with ideas, but with the great realities of our era. I hope the reader will come to a greater appreciation of Mao and the Chinese revolution. More importantly, I hope that we come to a new awareness of the ethical choices we face in a world of oppression and struggle.

NOTES

1. SW IV, p. 454.
2. SW III, p. 178.

CHAPTER 1

A FIGHTER'S PHILOSOPHY

Mao Zedong's philosophy was fashioned in the midst of war, revolution, and struggle. It is oriented to the task of political analysis and action for the revolutionary transformation of persons and society. It exemplifies what Karl Marx felt the role of philosophy to be, that is, to expose the causes of alienation and oppression through political criticism.[1] "The philosophers have only *interpreted* the world in various ways," wrote Marx; "the point, however, is to *change* it."[2]

Struggle against the opponents of revolution, in order to change the world, is central to Mao's philosophy. Stuart Schram has said that "Mao was a fighter, and a fighter requires enemies."[3] This is true, but it could be taken to mean that Mao went looking for enemies to satisfy the needs of a combative personality. It would be more to the point to say that the Chinese people were suffering and needed a fighter with a fighter's philosophy. One of Mao's earliest writings begins with these words: "Who are our enemies? Who are our friends? This is a question of the first importance for the revolution."[4] Mao did think in terms of enemies, but this was an expression of concern for the victims of oppression.

Here I will first discuss the situation of suffering that aroused people to revolutionary action. The struggle itself, which resulted in the liberation and revitalization of Chinese society, will also be considered. Since the victory of the revolution did not mean the end of struggle, however, attention will be given to the continuing struggle in the People's Republic.

This continuing struggle is referred to as the necessity to choose one of "two roads"—capitalist or socialist. A Communist victory did not mean that a new, unselfish, and nonexploitative society had been created overnight. Some people will still choose "the capitalist road" by seeking special privileges for themselves. The Great Proletarian Cultural Revolution of the late 1960s will be discussed as a dramatic development in this "two-road struggle."

The object of discussing the struggle before and after the revolutionary victory of 1949 is not to give a detailed historical account, which is available in other places, but to view the social situation with which Mao's thought interacted. Mao's thought is both a product of this struggle and a guiding force in it.

Three aspects of Mao's philosophy will be considered. These are his theory of contradiction, his sense of the just cause of the oppressed, and his vision of human destiny. All three aspects are closely related to the struggle ethic.

A Time for Revolution

At the time of Mao Zedong's birth in 1893 the Qing (Ching) dynasty was disintegrating. Foreign powers had made deep intrusions on China's sovereignty. Sun Yat-sen's revolution of 1911 did not unify the country but led to a period of warlordism and continued humiliation of China at the hands of foreign powers.

There are many accounts of the misery suffered by the Chinese people during the first half of the twentieth century.[5] Rather than recount statistics I will relate two cases which give an idea of the desperation of many Chinese people. The first is from a foreign observer, the second from contemporary Chinese sources.

Lucien Bianco gives several accounts of the agony of prerevolutionary China in a chapter on the social causes of the revolution.[6] One of these is taken from the 1931 letters of a foreign doctor working in Jiangxi:

Another desperate case that we treated for nothing [was] that of a young man who looked like a skeleton. One would say there was nothing but skin on his bones. . . . His family was so poor that they had been obliged to sell him. . . . He was accordingly sent . . . to a family that had no sons. When, six years later, a son was finally born, the new family simply threw him out. And the poverty is so great in the region that one month spent begging and homeless brought him to death's door.[7]

Bianco notes that it was not inhumane motivation but the brutalizing effects of poverty that led first to the sale of the child, then to his expulsion from the second home.

A second story is that of Lei Feng, a name now known throughout China since he became something of a folk hero after his death in 1962.[8] Lei Feng's early years symbolize the suffering before liberation, as his later years, which will be described further on, symbolize the transformation which came as a result of the revolution. The details of his life story may have been exaggerated somewhat, as hero stories tend to be.

Lei Feng was born in central China in 1940. When he was four years old his father was killed by the Japanese. In the next two years the rest of his family also died—his twelve-year-old brother from an accident in the factory where he worked, his younger brother from privation, and his mother by suicide after being raped by the landlord in whose house she had taken up employment as a servant.

As a six-year-old orphan, Lei Feng tended pigs for a landlord and slept in a hut with the pigs. His only pay was some coarse rice, which he cooked in a broken pot on an open fire. When one day the landlord's dog got Lei Feng's rice, the boy reacted by hitting the dog with a stick. This angered the landlord, who then hacked Lei Feng's arm three times with a knife and sent him off.

For the next few years the boy eked out a living collecting firewood in the forest. He was near death when his village was liberated in 1949. The leader of the new peasants' association found the nine-year-old boy sleeping in an abandoned temple in the forest.

These two cases, which are only representative, indicate the reality of human suffering which formed the backdrop of the struggle against those who caused such suffering. The desire for national salvation and independence was shared by many, including Mao.

Mao was twenty-five years old when the May Fourth Movement in 1919 sent revolutionary tremors throughout the nation, as students, workers, and tradesmen demonstrated against the betrayal of China's interests at the treaty conference in Versailles. Two years later, in 1921, Mao was one of the dozen delegates to the secret meeting in Shanghai at which the Communist Party of China was launched.

Over the next fifteen years Mao was active in organizing peasants in Hunan, his native province, and in establishing a revolutionary army at the mountain stronghold, Jinggang Shan. Hounded by Chiang Kai-shek's forces, the Red Army made its now legendary Long March across six thousand miles of rugged terrain in interior China.[9] Those who survived, with many others who joined them, carved out a base in a remote area of Yanan, from which the struggle continued. War raged on for more than a dozen years, against both Japanese occupation and counter-revolutionary Chinese forces.

In the course of these struggles Marxism came to be seen by Mao and others as the best guide to revolutionary action. Mao wrote:

For a hundred years, the finest sons and daughters of the disaster-ridden Chinese nation fought and sacrificed their lives, one stepping into the breach as another fell, in quest of the truth that would save the country and the people. This moves us to song and tears. But it was only after World War I and the October Revolution that we found Marxism-Leninism, the best of truths, the best of weapons for the liberation of our nation.[10]

Mao's philosophy of struggle grew out of the conditions of suffering and revolution in China and out of his understanding of Marxism.

Liberation

There were thirty years of war, hardship, planning, and struggle from the May Fourth Movement of 1919 until the

Communist victory in 1949. Many in the West saw the events of 1949 as the "fall" of China or the "loss" of China. In Peking, however, Mao declared the establishment of the People's Republic of China on October 1, 1949, with the words: "The Chinese people have stood up!" No matter how one judges the ensuing record of the People's Republic of China, the nation achieved unity and peace for the first time in a century. National integrity was restored and the moral life of the nation revitalized.

One can gain a sense of what the experience of renewal meant for the Chinese by looking again at the story of Lei Feng. After being found in the temple, Lei Feng was hospitalized for a short time, then was taken into the household of the peasants' association leader who had found him. At Lunar New Year he had his first experience of a family celebration with gifts, new clothes, and firecrackers. He was so moved he said to the peasant leader, "You are my savior." But the old peasant is reported to have replied, "No, child, Chairman Mao and the Liberation Army are our saviors."

Lei Feng participated in the land reform movement of the early 1950s. At an accusation rally he recalled the wrongs that had been done to him by the landlord. He jumped up onto the platform, seized the landlord by the collar with the scarred arm that the landlord had hacked, and told his fellow villagers how he had suffered. The landlord was sentenced to death. The boy witnessed the execution, ". . . which thus avenged him and all those who had suffered as he had."

Lei Feng, as an orphan, was given a free education, including free books. When he was older he volunteered to become a soldier in the People's Liberation Army. There, according to his diary which was found after his death and according to the accounts of others, he set an example as a selfless soldier seeking always to serve the people, "fearing neither hardship nor death."

The starved and dying Lei Feng of 1949 is a dramatic symbol of the Chinese people and their condition. The grateful Lei Feng of 1950 symbolizes the people who came to feel that Chairman Mao, the Communist Party, and the Liberation Army were their saviors. The vengeful Lei Feng grabbing the landlord with his scarred arm represents the peasants' new courage to retaliate against those who had oppressed them for so long. The suffering of Lei Feng's family lends legitimacy to the landlord executions. The selfless soldier which Lei Feng became represents the new person of the postliberation period.

A Revitalization Movement

Revolution and liberation in China can be regarded as a movement of revitalization. Certain features are common to revitalization movements of many kinds. It is possible to understand and appreciate these common features quite apart from any political judgment one may make about the revolution.

Anthony F. C. Wallace defines a revitalization movement as "a deliberate, organized, conscious effort by members of a society to construct a more satisfying culture."[11] Included in Wallace's description are various religious and political movements. (He makes particular reference to the Russian revolution, but China's experience is not covered in his study.)

When an established order breaks down, according to Wallace, there is a period of "cultural distortion." In these circumstances a revitalization movement may arise, providing a new world view and led by a charismatic leader. If successful it will lead to cultural transformation and then to routinization. Although Wallace covers other points, these features are relevant to China: cultural breakdown, new world view, charismatic leader, transformation and routinization.

Social and cultural breakdown may result from a variety of natural and political causes: climatic changes, epidemics, political subordination, military defeat, economic distress, or other destructive developments. Cultural distortion manifests itself in psychological and behavioral abnormalities such as alcoholism, intragroup violence, disregard for sexual mores, indolence, depression, self-reproach, and passivity. When one looks at the history of China in the century before liberation it is possible to identify many instances of cultural distortion.

This may explain the apparent inhumanity of some of the interpersonal relations.

The Communist revolution, as a revitalization movement, developed a new world view. Wallace says there are three possibilities for the development of a new world view: a revival of traditional culture, importation of a foreign cultural system, or the projection of a totally new "utopian" cultural system to be realized in the future. One can find elements of all three in Mao's thought. There is a combination of a foreign system, Marxism-Leninism, with traditional themes of Chinese culture. There is also a projection of a "new person and new society" to be realized fully only in the distant future.

Mao adapted Marxism and other foreign ideas in a manner which he felt suited China's conditions.[12] Wholesale Westernization was to be avoided, however. It was necessary to integrate properly the truth of Marxism with the concrete practice of the Chinese revolution. Even a Marxist China would have a distinctly Chinese cultural form.[13] Mao wrote:

For the Chinese Communists who are part of the great Chinese nation, flesh of its flesh and blood of its blood, any talk about Marxism in isolation from China's characteristics is merely Marxism in the abstract. . . . Foreign stereotypes must be abolished, there must be less singing of empty, abstract tunes, and dogmatism must be laid to rest; they must be replaced by the fresh, lively Chinese style and spirit which the common people of China love.[14]

A charismatic prophetic leader usually emerges in a revitalization movement, according to Wallace. Realizing this general phenomenon may make it easier to put into perspective the special position held by Mao in China. Wallace says that in a revitalization movement the leader is treated with great veneration as the embodiment of the hopes and dreams of the people. One may not favor personality cults yet still understand how they may arise from the psychological and social conditions that prevail.

Mao has been praised as a moral teacher and charismatic leader. A 1945 Party resolution said that Mao had "creatively applied the scientific theory of Marxism-Leninism, the acme of

human wisdom, to China. . . . [15] Two decades later, during the
Cultural Revolution, veneration of Mao reached cultic propor-
tions, with phrases like the following becoming common:
"The revolutionary people the world over have boundless
love for, boundless faith in, and boundless worship for Mao
Tse-tung Thought."[16] For a period, there was a proliferation
of statues, portraits, and badges bearing Mao's image.

The extremes of the Mao cult were an aberration and have
been checked. The more normal view is that Mao was a leader
produced by the people and Party. As the popular song in
China puts it: "Red is the East, rises the sun, *China has brought
forth* a Mao Tse-tung."[17] Mao himself has said that "the people
alone are the motive force in the making of world history."[18]

Mao reflected on the extremes of the personality cult
in what seems to have been a healthy manner. The late Edgar
Snow, while not quoting directly, reported on his conversation
with Mao in 1970 on this topic:

Of course the personality cult had been overdone. Today, things were
different. It was hard, the Chairman said, for people to overcome the
habits of 3,000 years of emperor-worshipping tradition. . . .

Other forms of worship had emerged. There were so many slogans,
pictures and plaster statues. The Red Guard had insisted that if you
didn't have those things around, you were being anti-Mao. In the past
few years there had been a need for some personality cult. Now there
was no such need and there should be a cooling down. . . .

There was always the desire to be worshipped and the desire to
worship. . . . There was bound to be some worship of the individual
and that applied to me too.

Chairman Mao has obviously pondered very much this phenomenon—the human need for and to worship, about gods and
God. . . . [19]

After a revitalization movement, with its new world view and
charismatic leadership, has been successful, Wallace says, a
new order is established and becomes routinized. China's case
would seem to bear this out to an extent, but the concept of
routinization is open to debate. First, the view of a movement

from order to breakdown to revitalization to routine new order could be taken as a cyclical theory of history with no real progress. Second, routinization could mean that when the new order is established the revitalizing process ceases. Both these implications of the routinization concept are in conflict with Mao's interpretation, which sees progress in history as a real possibility and continuous revolution as necessary for further progress.

Other questions could be raised about Wallace's study in relationship to China. A clearer distinction should be made between religious movements of revitalization, which do not usually include plans for political and economic transformation, and a Marxist revolution, which does. Also, Wallace does not face squarely the issues of imperialism and oppression which cause "cultural breakdown."[20] Nevertheless, his study has useful insights into the world view and charismatic leadership of a revolutionary movement.

The Capitalist Road and the Socialist Road

The years since the victory of the revolution in China have been marked by a succession of campaigns and movements to extend and deepen the revolutionary process, in contrast to what Wallace seems to mean by routinization. These included the land reform movement, anticorruption campaigns, the development of agricultural cooperatives and later communes, the Great Leap Forward, the Socialist Education Movement, and the Great Proletarian Cultural Revolution.[21] This last one, the Cultural Revolution, perhaps most characteristic of the spirit of continued struggle, will be discussed in the next section of this chapter.

The liberation of 1949 was not seen as the culmination of the revolution, but as the beginning of a journey. In that year Mao wrote:

Twenty-eight years of our Party are a long period, in which we have accomplished only one thing—we have won basic victory in the revolutionary war. This calls for celebration, because it is the people's victory, because it is a victory in a country as large as China. But we still have much work to do; to use the analogy of a journey, our past work is only the first step in a long march of ten thousand *li*.[22]

The image of a journey is significant both because it suggests a continuing process and because it raises the question of which road will be followed.

The various campaigns and movements are perceived by the Chinese as a process of struggle between the capitalist and the socialist roads. The shift of concern from capitalists to "capitalist roaders" is subtle but important. In socialist China there are no more capitalists. There are many "revisionists," however, persons who make choices in the economic, social, political, and cultural fields which would lead to the restoration of capitalism by cumulative effect if left unchecked. This means that all daily-life decisions need to be considered on the basis of whether they contribute to the socialist public good or to private and selfish "capitalist" interests.

The capitalist roader or revisionist is one who makes an easy compromise with selfishness. Several persons may act in collusion for personal gain. Such a grouping would be a revisionist structure, using the name of socialism but serving a privileged group.

Other characteristics of the capitalist roader are giving high priority to individual material incentives; having a bureaucratic disdain for the common people; looking down on physical labor; deferring human values for the sake of economic growth; being unwilling to try new things for fear of risk to personal position; and refusing to recognize that struggle between those with greater privilege and those with less is a continuing problem.

Those who follow the socialist road, on the contrary, persevere in the struggle against selfishness and social privilege. They emphasize the incentive of service, identify with ordinary people, and participate in physical labor. Revolutionary human goals are placed above purely economic goals, but even greater development is anticipated through the enthusiastic participation of all the people. Those who take the socialist road have the spirit of daring and are willing to experiment. They also recognize the need to struggle against privileged social strata in order to preserve the gains of the revolution.

The socialist road and the capitalist road represent two different approaches to development. The socialist path puts primary emphasis on people's participation. Economic construction is served by programs of mass health care and education, the development of "working class intellectuals," and a spirit of discovery and inventiveness among peasants and workers, leading to an "emancipation of productive forces" and to a rich material and cultural life for all the people.[23]

Capitalist roaders put primary emphasis on technology. In a 1959 speech, Liu Shaoqi (who was branded the leading capitalist roader some years later) made the statement that China's most serious problem is technological backwardness. Others immediately countered that this statement should not be taken to mean that "the struggle between two roads" could be de-emphasized. To overlook the profound social struggle at the heart of the technological revolution would open the way for capitalist tendencies.[24]

That intense social and personal struggle continues after the victory of the revolution is the clear implication of the capitalist road concept. Taking this road is a moral danger faced by each person. A Communist Party member can be a capitalist roader. Such persons scramble for position and gain, join the Party for the sake of improving their opportunities, and take public property for their private possession. Such behavior continues down to the present.[25]

Not only can a Party member be a capitalist roader, the head of state Liu Shaoqi was even accused of this error. In the early 1960s the lines were drawn between those who saw technological backwardness as China's greatest problem and those who put primary emphasis on "the struggle between the socialist road and the capitalist road."[26] The stage was set for the Cultural Revolution.

The Cultural Revolution

The Great Proletarian Cultural Revolution (hereafter cited: Cultural Revolution), one of the most dramatic social movements of the twentieth century, brought many of the issues of the two-road struggle into sharp focus. There is still a great deal of controversy about the goals, methods, and meaning of the movement. Volumes of documents and analyses line the walls of China libraries.[27] At its height schools were closed, millions of student Red Guards massed for rallies in Peking and travelled free on trains throughout the country, attacking revisionists or capitalist roaders. Eventually the army was brought in to quell the violent factional fighting that broke out.

An article by Yao Wenyuan, a young Party theoretician, signalled the beginning of the Cultural Revolution in late 1965. The article was a critique of a drama which contained a veiled attack on Mao and socialist road policies. Liu Shaoqi and his group had such complete control of Peking and national media that publication of the article was blocked everywhere but in Shanghai. Eventually the Cultural Revolution led to the overthrow of Liu and others close to him.

According to Chinese sources the Cultural Revolution was initiated and led by Chairman Mao. It was a mass mobilization of people to seize power from the new class of bureaucrats who were using their power to lead China down the capitalist road. The Cultural Revolution was hailed as an epoch-making breakthrough in the development of Marxist theory.[28]

In fact, the issues at stake in the Cultural Revolution were not totally new, although the intensity and scope of the struggle was unprecedented. Four issues will be considered at this point: technocratic power, disparity of income, special privileges of top leaders, and special schools for children of these leaders. In later chapters other aspects of the Cultural Revolution will be discussed: the problem of selfishness and the need to re-educate leaders in chapter 3; Cadre Schools, the call for renewal of revolutionary vitality, and self-criticism in chapter 4; and the debate on liberal values in chapter 5.

The issue of *technocratic power* was already present in the earlier two-road struggle. Those who felt that technology was the crucial problem for China tended to give special place to those with expertise, regardless of their commitment to social goals. According to his accusers, Liu Shaoqi stressed only "production, mechanization, and material incentives." Workers were simply to bury themselves in production instead of participating fully in the decision-making process and sharing fully in the new culture.

The socialist line of Mao urged the workers to struggle against the small group of experts who were running the factories. Technological improvements were necessary, but this should not preclude ordinary workers retaining political power and participating actively in management.[29] As the Cultural Revolution progressed and workers gained more scope for initiative, it was claimed that efficiency increased and technological innovations were more successful.[30] The theory of the Cultural Revolution is that an authoritarian bureaucracy, even using a system of wage and bonus incentives, leads to worker passivity; whereas a system which de-emphasizes material incentives, but in which the workers participate with full dignity and power, will be both more humane and more productive.

The question of *income disparity* is closely related to the above, and was also not new with the Cultural Revolution. The capitalist road policy was to give greater rewards for harder or more skillful work. The Maoist position was not that income differentials could be eliminated at this stage of history, but that they should be kept in check and not allowed to increase, and should be gradually eliminated as the society moved toward greater productivity and genuine communism. The capitalist roaders, by increasing material incentives with the hope of thereby increasing production, gave free reign to selfish motivations. This led people to think primarily of increasing their personal wealth. Unchecked, the disparities would increase and the class differences, which a bloody revolution had been fought to eliminate, would re-emerge.

Mao's view was not "utopian" in the negative sense. He did not assume that all people would suddenly start to live unselfishly. His emphasis on continued struggle was precisely meant to control renascent self-interest. He did not expect to establish absolute egalitarianism nor to overcome completely all selfish tendencies. He did feel that permanent struggle was necessary to keep these tendencies from taking over completely.

Gross *special privilege* for high-ranking officials was another issue of the Cultural Revolution. An easy tolerance of such privilege went hand in glove with the authoritarian technocratic mentality. For example, one Red Guard report exposed a plush club in Peking that was started in the late 1950s, the construction proceeding even during the so-called "three hard years" (1959–61), when national shortages required belt-tightening throughout the country. The club complex included carpeted rooms, dance halls, a heated swimming pool, bowling alleys, a billiard room, and a staff of girl attendants.[31] The Maoists were not against enjoyment, but against an attitude which allowed luxury for some while others faced adversity.

The question of *education* was one of the most fiercely contested issues of the Cultural Revolution. The special privileges of some officials were being made hereditary by the introduction of exclusive schools. This would allow their children to move directly into universities and on to "good jobs."[32] Liu Shaoqi is reported to have backed this two-track educational policy, providing minimal education for most children while giving university-oriented training to a small elite.[33]

As a result of the Cultural Revolution the university system has been modified. High school graduates go to work in farms or factories for at least two years. The work units nominate young people for university placement. Nominees are screened by the universities before entry. During their university training, students continue to spend time in physical labor. When their training has ended they are expected to return to their work units to use their new skills there.

The Cultural Revolution was not without its shortcomings. We have already mentioned the factional disputes which sometimes ended in pitched battles requiring military intervention. People were killed. There were periods of anarchism when the rejection of capitalist roaders moved to a rejection of all order and discipline.

Another negative phenomenon of the Cultural Revolution was the development of an extreme Mao cult. Where the capitalist road had given priority to technological expertise rather than people's participation, "Maoist fundamentalism" gave priority to a superficial mastery of Mao's thought. A person was judged by the number of Mao quotes memorized, the statues and portraits displayed, and the rhetoric mastered. It is a credit to the Chinese that they came to see that the impact of this cultism was just as authoritarian and divorced from the realities of the life of workers and peasants as was the capitalist road mentality.

In spite of its shortcomings, the Cultural Revolution went a long way in confronting the issues of people's power and participation. The struggle continues, and new movements and campaigns in the 1970s grapple with issues of income, life style, the educational system, leadership, and power—in short, with how to move closer to a society in which all persons work and all have access to cultural and social resources.

The long struggle from the days of Jinggang Shan and Yanan to the Cultural Revolution and its aftermath constitutes the milieu with which Mao's thought interacted. As suggested at the beginning of the chapter, Mao's thought was both influenced by, and had tremendous impact on, this struggle process. In the next section some of the themes of Mao's thought will be considered.

Themes in Mao's Philosophy

Mao's long involvement in the development of revolutionary strategy, military tactics, and social restructuring resulted in a philosophy geared to practical concerns. The dimension of struggle in Mao's thought is not simply a theory about conflict but reflects a whole style of life and action.

Mao's thought is action-oriented and he approaches Marx on those terms. According to Mao Marxism should not be considered a set of dogmas but a guide to action. Studying Marxism means mastering the art of revolution, not simply learning terms and phrases.[34] Mao expresses contempt for those who revere Marxism but do not put it to use.[35] If you want to know the taste of a pear, Mao says, you must eat the pear; if you want to know the meaning of revolution, you must take part in revolution.[36]

Mao responded to the charge that his philosophy was nothing more than a philosophy of struggle by saying that this was exactly the kind of philosophy China needed.[37] For the study of the struggle ethic, three aspects of Mao's philosophy of struggle are particularly important. These are his theories of contradiction, justice, and human destiny, to which we now turn. For a more comprehensive view of Mao's thinking one should consult his essays and various secondary sources.[38]

The theory of contradiction. The theory of contradiction is central to Mao's thought. It has roots both in Marxism and Chinese tradition.[39] Contradiction means the struggle of opposing forces within an entity. In Mao's view such struggle characterizes all natural and social phenomena. Even when things appear to be in a state of harmony or equilibrium they are going through a process of gradual or "quantitative" change. When unity or harmony is destroyed the thing can be said to be in a state of rapid "qualitative" change. Unity and harmony and equilibrium are relative and temporary, but the struggle of opposites in any given thing is absolute.[40]

For example, a chair, setting in a room, appears to be unchanging, but in fact it is aging or decaying. Quantitative change is taking place. If the chair caught fire, a rapid, qualitative change would take place. In either condition there is change, which Mao sees as the struggle of opposites within the thing.

The important point for this study is how the theory of contradiction relates to individual humans and groups. Contradiction, or the struggle of opposing forces, is ubiquitous, absolute, and unconditional. The whole universe and everything in it is in a state of struggle. This applies to human life as well. All societies are characterized by struggle and contradiction. Each person's thought is in a state of permanent struggle also.[41] Issues of social struggle will be treated more fully in chapter 2, and thought struggle in chapter 3. A few further points on human struggle will be made here.

Mao makes a distinction between two different types of social contradiction. One is the struggle between "people" and "enemy" (terms that will be explained more fully in the following chapter), which Mao calls antagonistic (*duikangxing*) contradictions. Such a contradiction can normally be resolved only through harsh, violent, revolutionary action. Antagonism may simmer in a society for a long time before revolution breaks out. Mao compared this process to a bomb, which is a "single entity" until a new element is added, ignition. Then an explosion, a qualitative change, takes place.

The second type is nonantagonistic. These are contradictions among the people. For example, there are possible conflicts of interest between workers and peasants, or between intellectuals and workers. Mao also recognizes tension between individual and social needs, between leaders and led, between government and people, in China today.[42] Such contradictions do not require violent revolutionary action for their resolution. They can be worked out peacefully by democratic methods of discussion, criticism, persuasion, and education.[43]

According to Mao's theory, it is possible, under certain circumstances, for nonantagonistic contradictions to become antagonistic.[44] If conflicts among the people are not handled properly and resolved in due course, a situation can develop in which violence would become necessary.[45] China feels that the special privileges of a new class in Russia have moved to such a point that only another revolution can resolve the present social conflict. They also feel that in China, in spite of outbreaks of factional fighting at the time, the Cultural Revolution checked the power of capitalist roaders before they could become entrenched to such a degree that another violent revolution would have been necessitated.

A conflict between the people and the enemy can sometimes be transformed into a nonantagonistic contradiction. After the victory of the revolution in China the old exploiting class continued to exist. Since power was in the hands of the proletariat, however, the conflict with the enemy class could be resolved peacefully.[46]

Mao's theory of social contradiction gives a clear and definite place to violent struggle. It also places limits on violence. Contradictions among the people are to be handled peacefully, and when the power of enemy classes has been broken, contradictions between people and enemy can also be dealt with in a nonviolent manner. Nevertheless, struggle and contradiction are permanent features of human society.

Mao's theory of justice. Although Mao sees contradiction in the human sphere as one dimension of a universal process, there is a crucial change in tone when he moves from discussion of natural phenomena to the human. In the natural world the development and resolution of contradictions is an impersonal, neutral process. In the human realm the process of struggle is one that moves in certain historical directions. The issue of justice arises, the issue of right and wrong, and the stand which persons take in relation to this issue. In this sense human struggle can be said to be a question of ethics, of the moral choices people make.

The theory of justice in Mao's thought is implied rather than stated systematically. It would be more nearly correct to say that Mao's writings exhibit a passion for justice, not a theory.

Justice is seen by Mao to be on the side of the masses. In the situation of suffering that Mao confronted in China, the problem was how to bring about a society in which the common people, the people at the grassroots, had full access to power, dignity, and to the resources of society. At one point Mao defined the masses as "all those who are oppressed, injured or fettered by imperialism, feudalism and bureaucrat capitalism, namely workers, peasants, soldiers, intellectuals, businessmen and other patriots."[47]

The term "masses" is more inclusive than the standard Marxist term "proletariat." It first meant all those who were oppressed by an exploitative system. After the revolution, when the exploitative system was overthrown in China, the term "masses" retained its importance since the question remained of how power can be exercised by the people, and how a new class of capitalist roaders can be kept from coming to power.

In the new system, organization and leadership are necessary. The Party exercises leadership.[48] The masses need to be led and educated. Leaders, however, should be subject to the criticisms of the masses and should be servants of the masses.[49]

The "mass line" is based on the belief that the common

people have great contributions to make, that they have wisdom and ability. Those who are fulfilling special functions, such as intellectuals, artists, Party and government officials, need to develop a spirit of identifying with the masses. How to develop such leadership is a continuing problem. Leaders, and students who are training to take up leadership positions, have to overcome the old idea that one studies and works in order to gain a position of personal privilege. Rather, one should serve, rely on, and identify with the masses of common workers and peasants.[50]

The passion for justice, which Mao inspires, led to a revolutionary struggle to overthrow systems of oppression and exploitation. It led to continuing struggle after the victory of revolution, against tendencies toward the reintroduction of special privilege for certain persons and groups. A concern for justice gives meaning to the continual process of contradiction in the human realm.

A vision of human destiny. Closely related to the concern for justice, which guides the process of contradiction in human life, is Mao's vision of the human destiny that is the goal of the struggle. A sense of destiny pervades Mao's writing. This is seen in his poetry. The following lines were written when he was a young and lonely revolutionary in the 1920s:

> Alone in the autumn cold
> I scan the river
> that flows northward.
>
> . . . .
>
> Bewildered by the immensity,
> I ask the vast grey earth:
> "Who decides men's destinies?"[51]

One also sees this sense of destiny in the way Mao describes human struggle in near cosmic terms. At one point he wrote of the forces of revolution and counterrevolution "locked in final struggle."[52] Later he wrote of the "unbridled violence of the forces of darkness" and saw these forces as "already in their death throes" with victory for China and "the entire world" approaching.[53] China was confronted with two possible destinies: "a destiny of light or a destiny of darkness." There were two prospects for the nation:

either a China which is independent, free, democratic, united, prosperous and strong, that is, a China full of light, a new China whose people have won liberation, or a China which is semi-colonial, semi-feudal, divided, poor and weak, that is the old China. . . . We must strive with all our might for a bright future, a destiny of light, and against a dark future, a destiny of darkness.[54]

Human action and struggle are required if there is to be any movement toward the realization of this vision of a bright future for China and for the world. In this sense Mao is a humanist, giving primary place to the human factor. Whatever is to be done, Mao says, is to be done by human beings. Ideas and action represent the dynamic role peculiar to human beings. Human consciousness and dynamic participation is a characteristic which distinguishes the human from all other beings.[55]

Does Mao believe that it is possible by human effort to achieve a society free of strife? Is his vision obtainable? Logically, it should be possible. Mao believes, however, that the process of resolving ever new contradictions is universal and eternal. Without contradiction and struggle, life itself would cease.

There is here an apparent inconsistency in Mao's thought, one which could be considered a paradox. Mao sees the present period in China as a time of socialism, in which the distinctions based on privilege are gradually eliminated. It will be followed by the classless society of communism. Nevertheless, contradiction and revolution will continue "forever" and "universally." The transition from socialism to communism is a revolution. Even in the communist classless society there will be stages of development, and the leap from one stage to the next will be a revolution, achieved through struggle. There will never be a time when conflict is eliminated. Revolution is permanent.[56]

Mao is grappling here with two sides of his thought which are, it seems, in paradoxical relationship to each other. On the one hand, there is movement toward the goal of a society of peace and justice. On the other, there is the understanding that contradiction and struggle are eternal.

The concept of permanent revolution keeps the vision of a classless society from being used to support the theory of reconciliation. Some voices in China say that conflicting forces can be reconciled without struggle after the victory of the revolution. Maoists fear that this approach leads to a lax attitude toward continuing effort to overcome class privilege in society. Concern is especially expressed over the possibility of capitalist roaders deceiving people with talk of reconciliation in order to offset struggle by the common people against new patterns of personal privilege which continue to emerge among the leaders.[57]

The starting point for Mao's ethic is contradiction and struggle. Mao's concern for justice and his vision of human destiny are essential for understanding his ethic and the meaning of struggle. The concepts of justice and destiny are distorted if they are used to support a theory of reconciliation without struggle. To be true to Mao's ethic it is necessary to affirm both the possibility of creating a new society of peace and justice, and paradoxically, to affirm that revolution is permanent, that life itself would cease if there were no continuing contradiction and struggle.

Conclusion

Mao's thought both grew out of and influenced the situation of China. Exploitation, suffering, and cultural breakdown were characteristic of the first half of this century in China. The response of the people was to struggle for national independence, liberation, and the overthrow of a corrupt system. This revolutionary response was successful and led to the revitalization of Chinese society. The process did not end there, however, and struggle has continued. The establishment of a new order, without a privileged class, still has not been achieved. The Cultural Revolution was the prime example of the continued effort to carry the revolution forward.

Three aspects of Mao's thought are intimately related to this continued process of struggle. His theory of contradiction and struggle is the starting point for the new ethic in China. This struggle has meaning and direction based on a passion for justice and the vision of a new society which can only be approached by human effort and unending revolution. Harmony and unity cannot be achieved, in Mao's view, by an attempt to reconcile conflicting forces. Contradictions must be resolved through struggle. The vision of a new society is in paradoxical relationship with the vision of permanent revolution.

It would not seem, from what has been said, that an ethic based on struggle is either unrealistically utopian or dehumanizing. Mao does not expect that a society in which everyone is unselfish and works only for the public good will be easily realized. So the emphasis on continued struggle is very realistic. Struggle, however, is not glorified for its own sake. The object of struggle is to check tendencies toward new, unfair privilege and to enable the masses of common people to attain and retain dignity and power.

The struggle ethic seems, therefore, to be both reasonable in its formulation and hopeful in its prospects. How this ethic works out in relation to social conflict, personal transformation, and lifestyle will be the subjects of the next three chapters.

NOTES

1. Karl Marx, "Contribution to the Critique of Hegel's Philosophy of Right," in *Marx and Engels on Religion* (New York: Schocken Books, 1964), p. 42.

2. Karl Marx, "Theses on Feuerbach," thesis XI, in *Marx and Engels on Religion*, p. 72; emphasis in the original.

3. Stuart Schram, *The Political Thought of Mao Tse-tung*, rev. ed. (New York: Praeger, 1969), p. 48.

4. SW I, p. 13.

5. For accounts of conditions in China prior to 1949, see Lucien Bianco, *Origins of the Chinese Revolution* (Stanford: Stanford University Press, 1971); William Hinton, *Fanshen* (New York: Monthly Review Press, 1966); and Jack Belden, *China Shakes the World* (New York: Monthly Review Press, 1970).

6. Bianco, *Origins,* pp. 82–107.

7. Ibid., p. 88.

8. The following account and quotations are taken from Ch'en Kuang-sheng, "Lei Feng—Soldier of Communism," in CY, nos. 5–6 (March 2, 1963), trans. in SCMM, no. 358 (April 1, 1963). There is some variation in details in another account by the same author, *Lei Feng, Chairman Mao's Good Fighter* (Peking: Foreign Languages Press, 1968).

9. For a vivid account of the Long March see Edgar Snow, *Red Star Over China* (New York: Grove Press, 1961), originally published in 1938.

10. SW III, p. 17.

11. Anthony F. C. Wallace, "Revitalization Movements," *American Anthropologist,* vol. 58 (April 1956), pp. 264–81. Also in the Bobbs-Merrill Reprint Series in the Social Sciences, A-230.

12. There is disagreement among scholars on the extent to which Mao's thought represents Marxism-Leninism, or is a new incarnation of traditional Chinese thought, or is "original." Fromm, in an attempt to elucidate what he considered to be "the real meaning of Marxist thought," relegated both Russian and Chinese developments to "pseudo-Marxism": Erich Fromm, *Marx's Concept of Man* (New York: Frederick Ungar, 1965), p. ix. Mills placed Mao among "new revisionists": C. Wright Mills, *The Marxists* (Harmondsworth: Penguin, 1962), ch. 12. A volume by Brandt, Schwarz, and Fairbank stated that much of Mao's writing showed "no originality" and simply used elements supplied by Lenin: Conrad Brandt, Benjamin Schwarz, and John K. Fairbank, *A Documentary History of Chinese Communism* (London: George Allen and Unwin, 1952), pp. 79, 261, 320.

13. SW II, pp. 380–81.

14. SW II, pp. 209–10.

15. Appendix: "Resolution on Certain Questions in the History of Our Party," SW III, p. 177.

16. Editorial, "Hold High the Great Red Banner of the Great Proletarian Cultural Revolution and Advance in the Wake of Victory," *Ta Kung Pao* (Peking), June 13, 1966, SCMP, no. 3733 (July 7, 1966), p. 16.

17. *Revolutionary Songs of China* (Peking: Foreign Languages Press, 1971), packet, emphasis added.

18. *Quotations from Chairman Mao Tsetung* (Peking: Foreign Languages Press, 1965), p. 118.

19. Edgar Snow, "A Conversation with Mao Tsetung," *Life,* April 30, 1971, pp. 46–47. No direct quotations are used in the article.

20. A study by Lanternari covering many of the same movements as Wallace gives a clearer moral perspective by using the term "oppressed" and by showing how Western imperial power gave rise to revitalization movements. "The birth of these movements can only be understood in the light of historical conditions relating to the colonial experiences and to the striving of subject peoples to become emancipated. . . . The purpose of this book is merely to underscore the indictment of Western civilization implicit in this cry for freedom" (Vittorio Lanternari, *The Religions of the Oppressed* [New York: Mentor Books, 1965], pp. vi–vii).

21. A number of these campaigns and movements are discussed briefly in

John King Fairbank. *The United States and China*, 3rd ed. (Cambridge: Harvard University Press, 1971), chaps. 15–17.

22. SW IV, p. 422. A *li* is a Chinese measure equivalent to about one-third of a mile.

23. Li Tsu, "Ideological Obstacles to Cultural Revolution," *Cheng-chih Hsueh-hsi (Political Study)*, no. 6 (June 13, 1958), ECMM, no. 138 (August 11, 1958), p. 24.

24. Wang Yun, "Have Contradictions Between the Two Roads Been Solved Already?" *Jen-wen Cha-chih (Journal of the Humanities)*, no. 1 (February 25, 1959), ECMM, no. 172 (June 15, 1959), pp. 1–3.

25. Chang Ch'un-ch'iao, "On Exercising All-round Dictatorship Over the Bourgeoisie," *RF*, no. 4 (April 1975), SPRCM, no. 819 (April 28, 1975), p. 10.

26. Huang Wen-yu, "There is Still Class Struggle," *Nan-fang Jih-pao (Southern Daily)*, May 28, 1973, SCMP, no. 3011 (July 3, 1963), pp. 3–6.

27. The following are useful collections of documents on the Cultural Revolution:
The Great Cultural Revolution in China (Hong Kong: Asia Research Centre, 1969).
The Great Power Struggle in China (Hong Kong: Asia Research Centre, 1969).
David Milton, Nancy Milton, and Franz Schurmann, eds., *People's China* (New York: Vintage Books, 1974).
Commentary on the Cultural Revolution is available in the following:
Michael Oksenberg et al., *The Cultural Revolution: 1967 in Review* (Ann Arbor: University of Michigan Press, 1968).
Joan Robinson, *The Cultural Revolution in China* (Harmondsworth: Penguin, 1969).

28. Commentator, "On Revolutionary Discipline and Revolutionary Authority of the Proletariat," *RF*, no. 3 (February 1, 1967), SCMM, no. 564 (February 20, 1967), pp. 1–4.

29. Mass Criticism and Repudiation Group for Policy Study of the Office of Ministry of Metallurgy (authors), "Mechanization Must Be Led by Revolutionization," *KM*, December 14, 1968, SCMM, no. 4336 (January 13, 1969), pp. 10–14.

30. Hsinhua News Agency, "Revolution Promotes Production," June 11, 1969, SCMP, no. 4439 (June 18, 1969), pp. 16–18.

31. "Uncovering the Inside Story of the So-called High-ranking Cadres Club at Yeng-feng Chia-tou," *T'ien An-men* (Peking), no. 2 (1967), SCMM, no. 576 (May 22, 1967), pp. 4–7.

32. SCMP, no. 4940 (May 17, 1967), p. 6.

33. Yenan Commune of the Ministry of Education (authors), "The Reactionary Nature of the 'Two-type' Educational System," PD, July 19, 1967, SCMP, no. 3996 (August 8, 1967), pp. 14–18.

34. SW II, p. 208.

35. SW II, p. 42.

36. FEP, p. 8.

56916

37. Mao's off-the-record comment was made in 1959 and recorded in the Red Guard publication *Jinggang Shan* (Peking), May 26, 1967.

38. The following are among the collections of writings of Mao Zedong in English translation:

Selected Works of Mao Tse-tung, 4 vols. (Peking: Foreign Languages Press, 1961–65).

Four Essays in Philosophy (Peking: Foreign Languages Press, 1966).

Stuart R. Schram, *The Political Thought of Mao Tse-tung*, rev. ed. (New York: Praeger, 1969); includes documents and commentary.

Stuart R. Schram, ed., *Mao Unrehearsed* (Harmondsworth: Penguin, 1974), reprinted in the United States under the title *Chairman Mao Speaks to the People*.

"Long Live Mao Tse-tung Thought," *CB*, no. 891, October 8, 1969 (Hong Kong: U.S. Consulate General).

"Collection of Statements by Mao Tse-tung (1956–1967)," *CB*, no. 892, October 21, 1969 (Hong Kong: U.S. Consulate General).

Miscellany of *Mao Tse-tung Thought (1949–1965)* (Washington D.C.: Joint Publications Research Service nos. 61269-1 & 2, February 20, 1974).

The following are particularly useful commentaries on Mao Zedong's thought and writing:

Jerome Ch'en, *Mao and the Chinese Revolution* (London: Oxford University Press, 1965).

Jerome Ch'en, *Mao* (Englewood Cliffs, New Jersey: Prentice Hall, 1969).

Stuart R. Schram, *Mao Tse-tung: A Biography* (New York: Pelican Books, 1967).

Benjamin I. Schwarz, *Chinese Communism and the Rise of Mao* (New York: Harper Torchbooks, 1967).

Frederic Wakeman, Jr., *History and Will: Philosophical Perspectives of Mao Tse-tung's Thought* (Berkeley: University of California Press, 1973).

39. Professor Niijima, of Japan's Waseda University, feels that Mao has given the Marxist theory of contradiction a special Chinese interpretation. "The way in which Mao uses the word 'contradiction' is completely different from the way in which the original Marxists used the same word. So I think that, above all, we must think of Mao's thought as being a special type of response, a uniquely Chinese way of thinking" (Atsuyeshi Niijima, "Fundamentals of Mao Tse-tung's Thought," *China and the Great Cultural Revolution* [Tokyo: World Student Christian Federation, Asia Office, 1969], p. 12).

James Hsiung's view is that Mao's theory of contradiction is based both on the tradition of Hegel, Marx, and Lenin, and on Chinese concepts of *yin* and *yang*, opposing forces that balance each other. The crucial difference, according to Hsiung, is that Mao sees progress from a lower stage to a higher stage through the resolution of contradictions and the development of new contradictions, whereas *yin-yang* theory is a circular process with continual new harmonizations of opposing forces (James Hsiung, *Ideology and Practice* [New York: Praeger, 1970]).

40. Mao wrote: "Such unity, solidarity, combination, harmony, balance, stalemate, deadlock, rest, constancy, equilibrium, solidity, attraction, etc., as we see in daily life, are all the appearances of things in the state of quantitative change. On the other hand, the dissolution of unity, that is, the destruction of

this solidarity, combination, harmony, balance, stalemate, deadlock, rest, constancy, equilibrium, solidity, and attraction, and the change of each into its opposite, are all the appearances of things in the state of qualitative change, the transformation of one process into another. Things are constantly transforming themselves from the first into the second state of motion; the struggle of opposites goes on in both states but the contradiction is resolved in the second state. That is why we say that the unity of opposites is conditional, temporary, and relative, while the struggle of mutually exclusive opposites is absolute."

He added: "We may add that the struggle between opposites permeates a process from beginning to end and makes one process transform itself into another, that it is ubiquitous, and that *struggle is therefore unconditional and absolute*" (FEP, pp. 67 and 68 [emphasis added]).

41. "The law of contradiction in things, that is, the law of the unity of opposites, is the fundamental law of nature and of society and therefore also the fundamental law of thought. It stands opposed to the metaphysical world outlook. It represents a great revolution in the history of human knowledge. According to dialectical materialism, contradiction is present in all processes of objectively existing things and of subjective thought and permeates all these processes from beginning to end; this is the universality and absoluteness of contradiction. Each contradiction and each of its aspects have their respective characteristics; this is the particularity and relativity of contradiction. In given conditions, opposites possess identity, and consequently can coexist in a single entity and can transform themselves into each other; this again is the particularity and relativity of contradiction. But the struggle of opposites is ceaseless, it goes on both when the opposites are coexisting and when they are transforming themselves into each other, and becomes especially conspicuous when they are transforming themselves into one another; this again is the universality and absoluteness of contradiction" (FEP, pp. 71–72).

42. FEP, pp. 80–81.

43. FEP, p. 86.

44. "Contradiction and struggle are universal and absolute, but the methods of resolving contradictions, that is, the forms of struggle, differ according to differences in the nature of the contradictions. Some contradictions are characterized by open antagonism, others are not. In accordance with the concrete development of things, some contradictions which were originally non-antagonistic develop into antagonistic ones, while others which were originally antagonistic develop into non-antagonistic ones" (FEP, p. 70).

45. FEP, p. 89.

46. FEP, p. 82.

47. SW IV, p. 207.

48. On the relationship of the masses and the Party, see Maurice Meisner, "Leninism and Maoism: Some Populist Perspectives in Marxism-Leninism in China," *China Quarterly* 45 (January-March 1971), pp. 2–36.

49. SW III, p. 71.

50. Editorial, "Receive Revolutionary Training in Socialist Education Movement," CY, no. 17 (September 1, 1964), SCMM, no. 443 (November 16, 1964), p. 34.

51. Michael Bulluck and Jerome Ch'en, trans., in Jerome Ch'en, *Mao and the Chinese Revolution* (New York: Oxford Press, 1967), pp. 320–21.

52. SW I, p. 14.

53. SW II, p. 378.

54. SW III, pp. 251–52.

55. SW IV, p. 151.

56. Stuart R. Schram, "Mao Tse-tung and the Theory of the Permanent Revolution, 1958–1969," *China Quarterly* 46 (April–June 1971), pp. 221–24. Another useful article on this theme is John Bryan Starr, "Conceptual Foundations of Mao Tsetung's Theory of Continuous Revolution," *Asian Survey* 11, no. 6 (June 1971): 610–28.

57. This issue was the center of a debate between those who emphasized the possibility of reconciling and harmonizing opposing forces (their catch phrase was "two combine into one"), and those who emphasized the struggle of opposing forces which goes on even when there is apparent unity (their phrase was "one divides into two"). Some of the articles related to this debate are:

Red Flag Reporter (author), "A New Polemic on the Philosophical Front: Report on Discussion of Comrade Yang Hsien-chen's Theory of Uniting Two into One," RF, no. 16 (August 31, 1964), SCMM, no. 434 (September 14, 1964).

Chin Jan, "Revolutionary Dialectics or Reconciliation of Contradictions," *Hsin Chien-she (New Construction),* no. 7 (July 20, 1964), SCMM, no. 434 (September 14, 1964).

Wang Sheng-t'ang, "Dividing One into Two Is the Ideological Weapon for Promoting Revolution in Production: Refuting the Fallacy of Combining Two into One," RF, nos. 23–24, combined issue (December 22, 1964), SCMM, no. 453 (January 25, 1965).

CHAPTER 2

THE STRUGGLE ETHIC
AND SOCIAL CONFLICT

In this chapter we will consider the implications of the struggle ethic for social conflict, both domestic and foreign. The position was taken in the previous chapter that Mao's ethic, based as it is on the primacy of struggle and a sense of justice and human destiny, is a reasonable and hopeful approach to the human situation. Is this a valid judgment? Does not the emphasis on struggle between the people and the enemy lead to a destructive use of violence? Does it not increase hatred and bitterness in society? Are not interhuman relations brutalized as the result of Mao's ethic? Has Mao's world view not led China to take an aggressive stand in foreign affairs?

The struggle ethic assumes that conflict in society is normative. It does not seek to create conflict, but to face it squarely. In a prerevolutionary society the contrast between those with power, wealth, privilege and those to whom these are denied is clear. The "people" are those who are oppressed and all who take their side, that is, the dispossessed and those who make an ethical choice to stand with the dispossessed.[1]

The "enemy" refers to the oppressors. Three forms or

categories can be discerned in Maoist discussions about the enemy. The enemy may be individual persons, social structures, or thought. Enemy individuals are said to be "real butchers with real butcher knives." If there is exploitation, oppression, racism, then there are exploiters, oppressors, racists. One cannot wish away the existence of those individuals who perpetrate injustice. The struggle against such enemies may be fierce and violent.

Enemy social structures, the second category of enemies, are the groups that exercise exploitative power, the enemy classes. Revolutionary struggle is aimed at destroying the enemy classes. This does not mean killing all the individuals who make up these classes. When the power of an enemy class has been broken, individuals within it may be reformed and won over to the side of the people.

The third kind of enemy, "enemy thought," is also to be destroyed, according to the struggle ethic. This kind of thought is characterized by selfishness, opportunism, the desire to live well at the expense of other people's misery. Such thought is rooted out by means of education, thought struggle, criticism, and self-criticism. This will be taken up in the next chapter.

Class struggle is this conflict between the people and the enemy, the oppressed and the oppressors. In an early essay Mao wrote of "four thick ropes binding the Chinese people." These were political authority, clan authority, religious authority, and the authority of the husband.[2] All these enemy structures are opposed in class struggle.

We will now turn to a more detailed look at the question of the struggle ethic in domestic affairs, and then, in the next section, in foreign affairs.

The Struggle Ethic and China's Domestic Policy and Practice

Mao's struggle ethic allows room for violence and animosity. The Chinese revolution was a violent one. The transition to a new social order was marked by bloodshed and terror. What was the extent of this violence? Is Mao's ethic the cause of inordinate bloodshed? Is the struggle ethic invalidated because of this violence? What kind of society emerged out of this violent revolutionary experience?

A violent revolution. Mao said that a revolution is not a dinner party but the violent overthrow of one class by another. The revolution in China was marked by long and bitter struggle from the days of Sun Yat-sen and Chiang Kai-shek down to the establishment of the new order. "Political power grows out of the barrel of a gun," according to Mao.[3] The Communists set up base areas, organized guerrilla units and regular armies, and finally won a military victory.

The transition to a new order saw landlord executions, thought reform movements, and acts of terror. An assessment by three Harvard scholars in the early 1950s was that:

Chinese Communism brings to the Chinese people the same grim prospect as Communism elsewhere—all the possibilities of slave labor on a massive scale for the state, of the coercion, torture and destruction of obdurate personalities, of children informing upon their parents, and neighbor spying upon neighbor. These possibilities are inherent in the further application of the Marxism-Leninism which has thus far so effectively inspired the revolutionary victory of the CCP[Chinese Communist Party]. Such evils are evidently the price of "socialist construction" and national strength under this system.[4]

Similar assessments continued to be made over the years. In 1959 a liberal Christian journal in America said that the first decade of "red revolution" in China had cost "15 or 20 million lives."[5] An article on the Op-Ed page of the *New York Times* in 1970 stated that Mao Zedong had "slaughtered, exiled, and imprisoned more than the total number of people killed and mutilated by Stalin and Hitler combined."[6]

In addition to landlord executions there were also harsh attempts to reform the thinking of those who resisted the revolution. Thought reform, or brainwashing, may be considered another form of terror. Some foreigners who were subjected to penal thought reform found it an excruciating experience.

Animosity also played a part in the transitional period.

There were "hate America" campaigns and other instances of anti-foreignism. University professors were often accused of having a "blind reverence" for America and the West. They were criticized for not being able to see clearly who was the enemy. American flags and personal possessions of American professors who had fled to Taiwan and the United States were being stored in some of the universities in the expectation that the foreigners would soon return.[7] Such lack of confidence in the new government was severely ridiculed. In this process animosity towards Western cultural imperialism was vehemently expressed.

Revolutionary violence in perspective. Although the military violence of the revolutionary war in China may be a problem for those who take a pacifist stand, it is difficult to see what nonviolent options were open to Mao and his followers. The communist revolution developed in a period of disorder, warlordism, and factional fighting. Sun Yat-sen and Chiang Kai-shek also led violent revolutionary struggles at an earlier period.

Mao's dictum about power from the barrel of a gun did not glorify violence; it simply recognized reality. In the same passage in which he spoke about the barrel of a gun Mao went on to say that it was only armed peasants and workers who would have a chance against the "armed bourgeoisie and landlords." With military power it had been possible to create a base area with schools, culture, and a new order. Mao concluded saying that he wanted to abolish war, but that "in order to get rid of the gun it is necessary to take up the gun."[8] Mao obviously is not a pacifist, but neither is he an advocate of unprincipled violence.

Mao believes that the will of the people is more important than weapons in determining victory.[9] Chiang Kai-shek had airplanes and tanks, the Communists only had "millet and rifles." Yet Mao was confident of victory because the people supported the revolution and because their cause was just.[10]

The terror of the transitional period must also be seen in perspective. Claims that ten to twenty million people were executed are exaggerations. Stuart Schram, using what he felt to be reliable sources, put the figure at about two million. This, he said, constituted 0.3 percent of the population. He commented:

This is not an enormously large toll for a social revolution of this magnitude, carried out in the wake of a long and cruel civil war which had taken even more victims on both sides. Moreover, there is no doubt that among the "counter-revolutionaries" thus repressed were included many individuals who had in fact engaged in clandestine activities against the regime.[11]

There was a real climate of terror in 1951, according to Schram, but the number of executions was far lower than the wild estimates of some critics. J. K. Fairbank, it may be noted, mentioned a figure that was even lower of "hundreds of thousands."[12]

In reflecting on executions of counter-revolutionaries several points can be made. There was violence in the old order, institutionalized violence. The account of Lei Feng is an example. The deaths of three of Lei's family members were directly related to the cruel inequities they experienced. The landlord condemned by Lei Feng cared more about his dog than the life of a young boy. The nationwide outpouring of people's animosity against the landlords and other oppressors resulted in a wave of terror that was almost impossible to prevent. Such a period of terror is characteristic of any revolution.[13] It does not seem to have been out of proportion in China. In addition, Chiang Kai-shek still had his army on Taiwan, supported by American power, and many of those condemned were working actively on Chiang's behalf to overthrow the new regime.

The terror of thought reform (or "brainwashing," to use the Cold War term) should also be seen in the light of this external threat. Armed conflict in Korea and American military presence in Taiwan and the Taiwan Straits certainly increased pressure on those intellectuals who may have sided with America against the new regime. Harsh thought reform seems to have been characteristic only of the early transitional period when the new government in China was consolidating its power. Some foreigners subjected to penal thought reform admitted after leaving China that they had been involved in espionage and did not see thought reform as an unjust or dehumanizing experience.[14] Thought reform will be discussed more fully in chapter 3.

It is in the context of armed conflict and the threat of American power that one should also see the so-called "hate America" campaigns. The term "hate America" was, in fact, rarely used by the Chinese. The term usually used was "oppose American imperialism." The United States was using its power to encircle China with bases and to isolate China diplomatically and economically. The U.S. and China were at war in Korea. The U.S. was also actively supporting the Chiang Kai-shek group in Taiwan as the legitimate government of China. It does not seem strange that under these conditions an effort was made to overcome remaining pro-American sympathies, especially among the many Chinese intellectuals who had been trained in America or by Americans in China.

The terror of executions, harsh thought reform, and hatred campaigns, which characterized the transitional period, were extremely unpleasant and no doubt resulted in some innocent suffering. This violence does not appear to have been out of all proportion, given the magnitude of the revolution and the external threats to the new regime. The experience of the early period tended to color assessments of the new order made by outside observers over the years. More recently, however, perceptions of China have changed greatly, and we are in a better position to judge the society that resulted from this violent revolution.

Changing perceptions of China's New Society. The détente between Washington and Peking and increasing access to China by foreign visitors have resulted in new assessments of Chinese life and society.[15] A series of articles by John S. Service is representative of these reappraisals.[16]

Service was born in China and lived there for a number of years before the Chinese revolution. He had an intimate knowledge of the old society. He saw the old China as a "troubled place," with warlordism, national disunity, war, "Japanese aggression, ruinous inflation, grinding poverty, natural disasters, callously rapacious rulers." The new society, achieved by a violent revolution, is free of derelicts, beggars, and starving children, according to Service. More important than material improvement is the quality of life he witnessed in a visit there in 1972:

Egalitarian confidence and self-assurance might be accompanied, one supposes, by some self-importance and arrogance. Actually, what one finds everywhere are courtesy, cheerful good humor and cooperative helpfulness.

The atmosphere is comfortable and relaxed and free of tensions. Everyone works hard. If any people have a work ethic, it must be the Chinese. But the pace is not frenetic. . . .

The police, unlike the past, are now unarmed—without even a stick. And, except for the men and women on traffic duty, they are few and inconspicuous. . . . Crime and robbery do not seem to be a problem. No longer are the walls around a new home or factory topped by jagged broken glass set in cement.

In all our travelling we never saw an adult strike a child; and only seldom did we hear a child cry.

This new civility may owe something to the example of a state and party that seem to prefer governing by persuasion and propaganda rather than by command and force. One wonders, though, if it does not also have some foundation in the much more comfortable, stable life enjoyed by most people, the broader sense of community that has been created, and the ending of the old, bitterly competitive scramble for a bare existence.

Mao's ethic, wrote Service, has led to a persistent drive against elitism and bureaucracy and to the elimination of the gap between mental and manual work and the chasm between intellectuals and workers. This ethic "rests on populist faith in the innate abilities and creativeness of the common people."

There is no simple description of life in China today that encompasses the complexities of that vast land. Service's report, based on a six-week visit, cannot be taken as the final word. It would be naive to contend that Chinese society is without tensions, problems, and dissatisfactions. The continued influx of émigrés to Hong Kong is an indication that some people are not content with their present situation. Violent clashes between contending political factions still break out from time to time.

If one compares the present situation with the institutionalized violence of prerevolutionary China—the violence that protected the wealth of landlords and factory owners, the terror of hunger and abject poverty, the conscription of young men into warlord armies, the abuse of illiterate peasants and their children—then it is possible to conclude that there has been a reduction of violence. The quality of life in China today, the sense of community, the decrease in crime, the absence of racial tension, the reduction of conflict between workers and owners, all compare favorably with China's past, and with some Western societies.

The struggle ethic and the reduction of violence. Does violence breed violence? Mao's ethic gives prominent place to revolutionary struggle. It assumes that social conflict is normative and in no way exceptional. Nevertheless, Mao's ethic, in spite of the terror of the transitional period of the early 1950s, led to a reduction of violence in China and to a society with a quality of life that compares favorably with other societies. How is this possible?

The struggle ethic is not a cause of violence. It does not purposely seek to create fighting and bloodshed. This ethic is based on a world view that acknowledges the reality of class struggle. It seeks to create a more just society by opposing the power of the oppressors with the power of the common people. It uses the armed strength of the workers and peasants to struggle against the armed power of the landlords and bourgeoisie. The violence of the oppressors comes first, and in the long run is more destructive than the revolutionary violence that opposes it. By eliminating this oppressive power, violence is reduced.

In the revolutionary society the vast chasm between rich and poor is overcome. This change rids society of the source of a great deal of violence. The gap between the very rich and the desperately poor is the cause of continuing conflict in a prerevolutionary society. When the gap is narrowed violence is reduced.

In the new society, where the oppressing class is no longer in power, a greater sense of security and social solidarity is enjoyed by the people. This leads to a new quality of interpersonal relationships. Harsh competition for survival or a fair share of society's resources is no longer necessary and people can relate to one another in a more cooperative and humane manner.

Vast differences in wealth in the old society fostered the desire to get rich. This mentality is one source of violent crime. When the differences are no longer present and the get-rich attitude is regularly criticized as antisocial, there is a reduction in such crime.

Petty thievery is also reduced by the changed social situation. As one example, in China's cities in the summertime, watermelons are stacked at street corners for sale during the day. At night they are left there with no fear of pilfering. With the new social equality and security there are no large segments of poor people who cannot afford to buy the melons. People also realize that no large profits are going to owners of private fruit companies. There is an understanding that the watermelons belong to the people.

The struggle ethic does not assume that in the new society all persons act unselfishly. There is a constant process of education, criticism, and self-criticism to keep these capitalist tendencies in check. Although this process is a form of social conflict, it is less violent than the struggle that results from some people being very rich and others very poor.

In domestic policy and practice the struggle ethic does not create violence, but leads to a reduction of violence.

The Struggle Ethic and China's Foreign Relations

Mao's vision of human destiny includes not only China but the world. Movement toward the goal of a new world order is through violent revolution against the forces of imperialism and exploitation. Do the worldwide implications of the struggle ethic lead China to an unprincipled and aggressive foreign policy? Is Mao's ethic a destructive factor in international rela-

tions? Is China's policy expansionist and a threat to world
peace? Is the struggle ethic of Mao to be condemned because
of the foreign policy and practice to which it leads?

The charges of Chinese military aggression. When the Liberation
Army was moving into South China, even before the People's
Republic of China was established, some observers feared that
the army would not stop at the border but continue right
through Southeast Asia.[17] It was assumed that China's foreign
policy would be expansionist. Over the next two decades, with
conflicts in Tibet, Korea, Quemoy, and on the Sino-Indian and
Sino-Soviet borders, many critics considered that China took
an irrationally aggressive role.

The Sino-Indian border war of 1962 is an interesting case
study of how China's international behavior was perceived. At
the time of this incident one American journal in an editorial
entitled "Help India!" said that China launched the attack.
The motivation for aggression, it was claimed, was that China
was falling behind India in development, was in competition
with India in ideology, and desired access to Indian oil in
Assam. The editorial expressed the hope that China would
become so bogged down in the war that the regime in Peking
would collapse.[18] China's alleged wanton aggression against
India contributed to the U.S. image of an expansionist China.
This view supported the U.S. policy of "containing" China.[19]

Nearly a decade after the border war this assessment of
China's role was reversed. J. K. Fairbank of Harvard wrote an
article in 1971 in which he said the blame for the war should be
put squarely on India. He based this view on Neville Maxwell's
book, *India's China War.* Maxwell had exposed an "astig-
matism," said Fairbank, which had distorted Indian and Western views of China. China's performance was shown to have
been "rational and reasonable" and India's performance
"steadily more unreasonable and irrational." The charge of
unprovoked Chinese aggression against India, a pillar of the
United States containment policy, had been completely refuted, according to Fairbank.[20]

The removal of one pillar does not bring the whole house
down, but the degree of distortion in the case of the Sino-

Indian border war must lead one to question other charges of Chinese aggression. As early as 1964 Australian scholar C.P. Fitzgerald had argued that China's actions in contiguous or border areas had been rational and were easily explicable without any reference to an aggressive ideology.[21] A Canadian pamphlet, written in 1965, succinctly refuted the accusation of Chinese aggression, arguing that China's behavior in each of the various incidents around its borders was reasonable and restrained.[22]

The charges of ideological expansionism. In 1971, even the United States Information Agency's journal, *Problems of Communism*, carried a debate on Chinese expansionism, suggesting that Chinese aggression was no longer an unquestioned assumption in official U.S. circles.[23]

In the debate in *Problems of Communism* Franz Michael took the position that China is aggressive, but changed the meaning of the term. He said that "in terms of traditional concepts of what constitutes aggressive international behavior" China is not expansionist. It has "no territorial ambitions beyond its present borders." He argued, however, that China practices expansionism in terms of the "spread of Communist world revolution."[24]

Taking the other side in the debate, Peter Van Ness held that not only is China not expansionist in the traditional sense, but that China was not practicing aggression through insurgency or wars of national liberation. Van Ness made his point on the grounds that China lacks the resources for carrying out such programs and, more importantly, that such expansionism would contradict "Maoist morality." This morality, wrote Van Ness, emphasized self-reliance and the need for any oppressed people to liberate themselves. He concluded: "Hence, one might say that the Maoist philosophical concept of international influence is not of the expansion of Chinese state power, but rather one of the successful diffusion of Maoist political virtue."[25]

Several things should be noted about this debate. First, Michael's position is that China has no territorial ambitions beyond its borders. His more negative view of Chinese actions would still support the point that China is not militarily aggressive. China's expansion amounts to an attempt to spread world revolution. Van Ness modifies this position to the point of saying that this is done by the diffusion of Maoist morality. The subtleties of this position are a long way from the accusations of blatant aggression made in earlier years.

Is the diffusion of Maoist morality aggression? If so, then the movement of any ideas across international boundaries would have to be considered expansionist. If this is the case, what nation is not aggressive?

A "realistic" view is that nations have three ways of relating with each other: diplomacy (including cultural and technical exchanges and sometimes war), trade, and subversion. Subversion, in addition to intelligence gathering, sabotage, and similar tactics, would include the spread and support of ideas which would weaken the system of authority in another country. There is international struggle for the "hearts and minds" of people. Serious issues of world view, morality, and politics are at stake in this struggle.

The question here is whether China's attempt at the "diffusion of Maoist political virtue" is aggressive. The answer is yes, but only in the sense that virtually all nations are aggressive. There are no grounds here for saying that Mao's ethic leads to a program that seeks control of other nations, increased territory, or the destruction of world peace and order.

China does support the right of people to struggle against oppression. Van Ness made the point that according to Maoist morality any oppressed people must be self-reliant and must liberate themselves. China's foreign policy is not "unprincipled." It is based on principles of peaceful coexistence and its judgment of what constitutes a just war.

The struggle ethic and China's principles of foreign relations. China has expressed support for the five principles of peaceful coexistence set out in the Bandung Conference of Afro-Asian States in 1955. These principles are:

1. Mutual respect for each other's territorial integrity and sovereignty;

2. Non-aggression;
3. Non-interference in each other's internal affairs;
4. Equality and mutual benefit; and
5. Peaceful co-existence.[26]

According to these principles China does not seek hegemony or the control of other countries or interfere in the internal affairs of other states.

While adhering to the principles of peaceful coexistence, China also supports the right of oppressed people to carry out revolution:

Peaceful coexistence refers to the relations between nations; revolution means the overthrow of oppressors as a class by the oppressed people within each country, while in the case of colonial and semicolonial countries, it is first and foremost a question of overthrowing alien oppressors, namely, the imperialists.[27]

Insofar as China believes in supporting revolutionary wars in other countries, there is an obvious tension with the principle of noninterference.

In the case of colonial and semicolonial countries, where an outside power is involved in maintaining an oppressive situation, China's aiding a liberation struggle could be defended as aiding a country to achieve independence. If no outside country is involved and China simply gives moral support to a revolutionary movement, then the question of interference would be quite limited. If armed support were given to a liberation movement in an independent country which was not being propped up by an outside country, then the principle of noninterference would be clearly broken.

The principle on which China bases its support for revolutions and wars of liberation is the theory of just war. Theories of just war have existed in the West for centuries. They have to do with the justifiable conditions under which a nation may go to war.[28] China's just war theory has apparently been developed independently of this Western tradition. It is closely related to the principles of the struggle ethic discussed in chapter 1, particularly the concept that in social struggle justice is on the side of the oppressed.

Mao's position is that a revolutionary class war is a just war.[29] It is legitimate for people to carry out a struggle against oppression. This principle was drawn on in a speech by the Chinese delegate to the 1974 conference on the Geneva Conventions on rules of war. He called for support for just wars, revolutionary wars. Specifically, he supported the position taken by many Third World countries that wars of national liberation should be given legal status. This would mean that liberation fighters would have the legal right to the same treatment accorded combatants under the present Geneva Conventions.[30]

A serious issue in international law is at stake here. More important is the political issue. If legal status is given to liberation fighters, then the struggle against colonialism and imperialism would be given new international political legitimacy.

On the basis of the principles of peaceful coexistence and the revolutionary just war theory, China's view of aggression is twofold. The use of military power for the purposes of oppression, establishing colonies, controlling other countries' economies, and setting up client states with no real support of the people would violate the just war theory. Establishing military bases and missile sites, sending large armies overseas, and interfering in the affairs of other countries would violate the principles of peaceful coexistence.

Has China put its foreign policy principles into practice? China has no foreign military bases or troops stationed overseas. It has not used military power to control the economies or affairs of other countries. China supports peoples' right to revolution and the justifiability of peoples of the Third World struggling for national independence and liberation.

China supports wars of national liberation by providing a framework for analyzing imperialism, by giving encouragement to liberation groups, by training personnel, and in some cases by giving material support. For example, China helped to supply Vietnamese liberation fighters. As Van Ness pointed out, China believes that people must be self-reliant and must liberate themselves. China does not use its troops to fight other people's wars.[31]

China accuses the United States of imperialism and aggression. From Mao's point of view American support of Chiang Kai-shek in China's civil war was unjustified interference in China's internal affairs.[32] Continued American military presence in Taiwan Province is also considered unjustifiable. From China's point of view the large number of American military bases overseas and the use of American troops in Vietnam's civil war are also cases of foreign aggression.

The United States and China differ on the just war theory. The U.S. delegate to the conference on the Geneva Conventions attacked the concept that wars of national liberation are just.[33] It is ironic that two centuries after the establishment of the United States through an anticolonial war of national liberation the U.S. position now denies the justification for such wars.

International relations are complex and constantly changing. "Principles" are sometimes stated for public consumption rather than as a guide to action. Charges of aggression are often for propaganda purposes. Nevertheless nations are guided to some extent by what they believe to be right and wrong. On one level, charges of American aggression and Chinese aggression can be judged in specific cases on accepted principles of national security and territorial integrity. On another level, such charges have to be seen in the context of questions such as imperialism, liberation, revolution, colonialism, economic neocolonialism, hegemonism, oppression, freedom, and democracy.

On the first level, some have argued that China's actions have been reasonable and rational and do not constitute aggression. This position is more generally accepted now than in the past, as the discussion above would indicate. Fairbank refutes charges of Chinese aggression on the India border. Both sides in the Michael-Van Ness debate agree that China has not sought territorial expansion. While some may not accept these arguments in all cases, it can at least be said that

China has not been guilty of gross and unrestrained aggression.

On the second level, the question is how one views the international struggle. China's view is that people have the right to carry out revolution against oppressive regimes and to fight wars of national liberation against colonial and hegemonic powers. Such struggles will obviously change world power relations. For those who wish to protect the status quo, support for such struggles is seen as aggressive. For those who feel that the poor nations of the world are suffering under imperialism, support for these struggles is honorable and just.

Do the international implications of Mao's struggle ethic lead to its invalidation? Has this ethic made China aggressive and a threat to world peace? The charges of wanton aggression and territorial ambition have been exaggerated. In general China's actions have been reasonable by world standards.

The struggle ethic does justify wars of liberation and revolution, on the basis of the right of people to oppose oppression. The issue of aggression in such instances can be judged only on an evaluation of the conditions of oppression and imperialism. Even in these situations, however, China takes the stand that people must achieve their own liberation. China has not fought wars of liberation in other countries; it supports peoples' right to revolution only where such struggles have already begun. Such an approach will be seen by some as a threat to world peace and order; others will see it as supporting justifiable resistance to an unjust status quo.

Conclusion

We have suggested that the struggle ethic is reasonable and hopeful. The theoretical basis of Mao's struggle ethic is a view of permanent social struggle, justice, and human destiny. Does the practice of the struggle ethic, in domestic and international conflicts, substantiate the claim that it is a reasonable and hopeful approach to the world?

It is my opinion that neither China's internal nor international policies and actions invalidate the struggle ethic. The policy of breaking down distinctions between rich and poor, privileged and unprivileged, and the resultant reduction of violence, is very reasonable. The awareness that new systems of privilege tend to emerge and must be struggled against makes the struggle ethic a hopeful one for the future. China's support for the principles of peaceful coexistence, its opposition to foreign military bases and to the policy of sending troops to fight in other people's wars, is also reasonable. China's support for the right of people to carry out revolution against oppression and to fight for national liberation is a hopeful approach to the future.

A reduction of violence does not mean Chinese society is without tensions or that suffering has been eliminated. Support by China of the principles of peaceful coexistence and of a just war does not mean that China will always act on those principles. Nevertheless, the positive developments that have resulted from the impact of the struggle ethic on Chinese policy and practice are worthy of appreciation by anyone concerned with the questions of international justice and the quality of interhuman relations.

NOTES

1. FEP, pp. 80–81.

2. SW I, p. 44.

3. SW II, pp. 224–25.

4. Conrad Brandt, Benjamin Schwartz, and John K. Fairbank, *A Documentary History of Chinese Communism* (London: George Allen and Unwin, 1952), p. 482.

5. Editorial, *Christian Century* 76, no. 41 (October 14, 1959):1173.

6. Bruno Shaw, "A Warning Against Mao," *New York Times*, November 13, 1970, Op-Ed page.

7. "Waste in Peking Universities," *Ta Kung Pao* (Hong Kong), March 7, 1952, SCMP, no. 293 (March 12, 1952), pp. 18–19.

8. SW II, pp. 224–25.

9. SW IV, p. 100.

10. SW IV, p. 101.

11. Stuart Schram, *Mao Tse-tung* (Harmondsworth: Penguin Books, 1966), pp. 267–68.

12. John K. Fairbank, *The United States and China* (Cambridge: Harvard University Press, 1958), p. 288.

13. For example, see Crane Brinton, *Anatomy of Revolution* (New York: Vintage Books, 1965).

14. See Allyn and Adele Rickett, *Prisoners of Liberation: Four Years in a Chinese Communist Prison* (Garden City: Anchor Books, 1973), first published in 1957.

15. For example, see the series of articles by Joseph Alsop in his "Matter of Fact" column after his visit to China. These appeared in the *San Francisco Chronicle* in December 1972 and January 1973. In addition the following visitors' accounts are instructive:
Bronson Clark, "Can Christians Learn from China," *China Notes* 9, no. 4 (Autumn 1971): 37–39.
Committee of Concerned Asian Scholars, *China! Inside the People's Republic* (New York: Bantam Books, 1972).
Harrison E. Salisbury, *To Peking and Beyond: A Report on the New Asia* (New York: Quadrangle Books, 1973).

16. John S. Service, "The Return of a Native: (I) That Old China was a Troubled Place," *New York Times*, January 24, 1972; "(III) Life in China is 'Obviously Better,' " *New York Times*, January 26, 1973; "(IV) 'China's Very Unstarchy Army,' " *New York Times*, January 27, 1972.

17. *Christian Century* 66, no. 28 (July 13, 1949): 837.

18. Editorial, *Christian Century* 79, no. 48 (November 28, 1962): 1439.

19. John K. Fairbank, "How Aggressive is China?" *New York Review* 16, no. 7 (April 22, 1971): 3–8.

20. Ibid.

46   *Love and Struggle in Mao's Thought*

21. C. P. Fitzgerald, *The Birth of Communist China* (Harmondsworth: Penguin Books, 1964), chaps. 8 and 9.

22. Charles W. Burchill, *Chinese Aggression: Myth or Menace?* (Vancouver: Study Group on China Policy, 1965).

23. Franz Michael, "A Design for Aggression," and Peter Van Ness, "Mao Tse-tung and Revolutionary 'Self-Reliance,' "*Problems of Communism* 20, nos. 1 and 2, combined issue (January-April 1971): 62–74.

24. Michael, "Design for Aggression," p. 63.

25. Van Ness, "Mao Tse-tung," pp. 73–74.

26. G. V. Ambekar and V. D. Divekar, eds., *Documents on China's Relations with South and Southeast Asia, 1949–1962* (Bombay: Allied Publishers Private Ltd., 1964), p. 7.

27. "Long Live Leninism," *Peking Review,* April 1960, in *Essential Works of Marxism,* ed. Arthur P. Mendel (New York: Bantam, 1965), p. 542.

28. For a brief discussion of the just war theory in the West, see "Just War," and "Peace and War," in John MacQuarrie, ed., *Dictionary of Christian Ethics* (Philadelphia: Westminster Press, 1967), and John Rawls, *A Theory of Justice* (London: Oxford University Press, 1972), pp. 379–82.

29. "War, this monster of mutual slaughter among men, will finally be eliminated by the progress of human society, and in the not too distant future too. But there is only one way to eliminate it and that is to oppose war with war, . . . to oppose counter-revolutionary class war with revolutionary class war. History only knows two kinds of war, just and unjust. . . . All counter-revolutionary wars are unjust, all revolutionary wars are just" (SW I, pp. 182–83).

30. Hsinhua News Agency, Geneva, March 6, 1974.

31. The participation of Chinese volunteers in the Korean War might be considered an exception, but I.C. Ohja argues that China's action there was to safeguard its national security and was not dissimilar to American action in the Cuban missile crisis (Isher C. Ohja, *Chinese Foreign Policy in an Age of Transition: The Politics of Cultural Despair* [Boston: Beacon Press, 1969], p. 73).

32. SW IV, pp. 425–32.

33. *Hong Kong Standard,* March 8, 1974.

CHAPTER 3

THE STRUGGLE ETHIC
AND PERSONAL
TRANSFORMATION

We now turn our attention from social to personal transformation. We have already suggested the significance of personal thought struggle for Maoists. We have seen that the "human factor," the thought and will and commitment of individuals, plays a central role in Mao's world view. Social revolution may be said to follow "inevitable laws of history," but this does not reduce the importance of personal decision.

Why are thought and will of such vital concern for Mao? Although social conditions and economic status shape a person's thought, it is also possible to make a moral decision that goes against one's class background. The poor peasant revolutionary can be corrupted and adopt the selfish attitude of a landlord. An upper middle-class intellectual can identify with the cause of the workers.

Not only is personal transformation possible, it is a necessary part of the revolutionary movement. The struggle ethic functions on the personal and the social plane simultaneously. Reform of society leads to reform of thought, and thought reform contributes to social progress. Degenerate thought corrupts social structures, which in turn foster further individual corruption.

Contradiction and struggle pervade not only nature and society but subjective thought as well. Each person, whether proletarian or bourgeois, revolutionary or reactionary, can progress by struggling against selfishness, arrogance, laziness, fear, and timidity. If constant, vigilant struggle is not maintained, then one will regress.

This means that no one can escape moral responsibility. Proletarians cannot assume a natural purity because they have been born poor. They, too, must struggle against the corrosive influences of the old, self-centered culture. Landlords cannot claim that they are exploiters because of the "fate" of having been born wealthy. They also have the opportunity of taking a moral stand on the side of the common people.

Struggle is ceaseless. In the context of personal transformation the struggle ethic means that there is no resting place. At each moment a person will either move forward or backward. There is no standing still. Every failure can be an occasion for self-pity, one form of selfishness, or for renewed effort. Every success can be an occasion for arrogance, another way of putting self first, or it can lead to further progress.

"It is easy to destroy thieves in the mountains, but it is difficult to destroy the enemies within our own hearts."[1] So wrote Wang Yangming, a philosopher of the Ming dynasty. His words were echoed centuries later when Mao Zedong wrote: "It is often more difficult to combat the enemies inside people's minds than to fight Japanese imperialism."[2] Mao's writings show a deep concern for this struggle that goes on in the mind of the individual.

Often Maoists refer to the soul and the transformation that can take place at the very depths of one's being. This deeply personal process is seen as one dimension of class struggle.

Class struggle goes on in the minds of human beings in their concrete social situations.

The attempt to transform persons in China is not without serious problems. Thought reform is the process which, in the 1950s, was labeled "brainwashing" by Western observers. To what extent are fears about brainwashing valid? Does the struggle ethic in the area of personal change give rise to thought control in China? Is the process of reform a de-humanizing one? Does it lead to bland conformity?

The term *thought reform (sixiang gaizao)* is sometimes trans-lated "ideological remolding." It is, in fact, a moral transforma-tion in which one comes to put the public or common good above personal interests. Although certain norms are assumed (individualism is bad, public-spiritedness is good) and tech-niques used (criticism and self-criticism in small group situa-tions), thought reform is not done to others but to oneself.[3]

The term *self-revolutionization (ziwo geming)* also refers to this continuing struggle to overcome self-centeredness. Thought reform is a process in which the individual is not a passive recipient but an active agent of self-revolutionization.

Self (si) used alone means "selfishness or private interests" in contrast to the interest of the whole people (another word for "self" is *zi*—see glossary). In this sense it carries negative conno-tations. "Self" stands as a barrier in one's personal struggle to achieve the transformation necessary to be able to function properly in a nonexploitative society. "Self" is an opponent in the class struggle carried out in the mind of an individual. Self-revolutionization means overcoming the narrow "self" or self-centeredness and moving beyond preoccupation with pri-vate concerns.

How can class struggle take place in a person's thought? According to Maoism, subjective thought reflects objective social conditions. Since there are different classes in society, a person's thought reflects influences from these various classes. A distinction is made between *class status (jieji chushen)* and *class stand (jieji-lichang)*. Class status or background is a given, since every person is of course born into one class or another. Class stand, as the term itself indicates, is the position one takes. Regardless of class status one can choose to stand either with the privileged or the oppressed. It is possible to stand with the workers and poor peasants, even if one comes from a privileged class. Similarly, a proletarian can betray his class and adopt bourgeois attitudes. Class status cannot be chosen; class stand can be.

This thought struggle is similar to the ethical choices facing anyone, the need to choose between good and evil. The significant factor in Mao's approach is that this internal conflict is seen as class struggle. This means that the struggle of the soul cannot be carried out in isolation from issues of social justice. Thought struggle is not an individual experience only. It takes place in a social context and has social consequences. Maoists are critical of those who assume that through study and self-cultivation, "behind closed doors," it is possible to achieve revolutionary purity.

The term *red (hong)* is used in the discussion of thought struggle. It means revolutionary commitment to the people and carries the moral connotation of selflessness. "Red" and "expert" are often paired. Expertise can be gained through study and experience. To acquire "redness" one must struggle on a deeper level to overcome individualism and self-centered attitudes. Redness is not a natural gift received through birth in the proletarian class nor is it an automatic attribute of revolutionary fighters. It can be attained and retained only through deep personal struggle.

Bourgeois (zichan jieji), in addition to referring to the capitalist class, takes on the moral connotation of evil. In contrast with proletarian redness, bourgeois stands for selfish individualism, living off the sweat of others, giving first place to narrow private interests. Even though the power of the capitalist class was broken in China in 1949, bourgeois attitudes continue to be a problem. Members of the capitalist class remain in the new society; the influence of the profit motive did not disappear overnight.

The selfish misuse of power by those who are supposed to be revolutionaries is also a continuing problem. *Revisionism (xiu-*

zhengzhuyi) refers to the world view of the new enemies who arise within the revolutionary ranks. Revisionists form a new structure of oppression, a new class enemy. They use Marxist language but in practice are concerned about building up power and privilege for their own special group. They become class enemies because of the moral choices they make about whom to serve.

Three ways of defining the enemy were listed in chapter 2: enemy individuals, enemy social structures, and enemy thought. This chapter on personal transformation centers on enemy thought. Attention will be given to the transformation of the thought of the bourgeoisie, both the exploiting classes as such and "petty-bourgeois" intellectuals. The latter are seen as a wavering group, not active exploiters, yet living off an exploitative system before the revolution. We will look at the question of transformation of revolutionaries themselves. Self-revolutionization, even for the ardent follower of Mao, is a permanent process.

Transformation of Landlords and the Bourgeoisie

The handling of class enemies and bourgeois intellectuals is an important question for the study of the struggle ethic. This is an area where many observers feel that China's practice has been questionable. Since animosity towards the enemy is approved and struggle affirmed, there is the danger that insensitivity to human life is fostered. Some persons might be looked upon simply as enemies to be destroyed.

In the struggle ethic capital punishment is not ruled out, but the position is taken that most persons can be transformed. Extensive use was made of capital punishment at the time of the revolutionary takeover. Mao said that a certain number of executions were necessary for the sake of establishing revolutionary order. He tried to limit this to "the handful of arch-criminals" who were "really guilty of the most heinous crimes." Capital punishment was to be carried out only after trial by people's courts and proper review by government committees.[4] We have already noted the controversy among observers over the extent to which execution was used in this period.

Mao said that indiscriminate killing was "entirely wrong" and if allowed to happen would result in loss of mass support for the Party. The landlords and rich peasants made up 10 percent of the rural population. They were seen as a group of people who could be molded to become productive members of the new society. "Our task is to abolish the feudal system," wrote Mao, "to wipe out the landlords as a class, not as individuals."[5]

Individuals, nevertheless, needed to transform their thought in order to be able to function in the new society. They could not continue on the basis of individualism and special privilege. Did such transformation mean forcing people to accept communist ideas? Did this violate their human rights? This question has to be seen in the context of the conflict between the liberal values of pluralism, individualism, and freedom of thought, and the revolutionary values of social discipline and unity, communalism, and selflessness for the sake of the people. The conflict of Maoism with liberal values will be discussed more fully in chapter 5.

From the Maoist viewpoint, thought reform is certainly not inhumane. On the contrary, it is because of their firm belief that people can change through thought reform that Maoists were hopeful that landlords, rich peasants, and bourgeois intellectuals could become productive members of the new socialist society.

Brainwashing. The very process of transforming enemies into ordinary citizens has been called brainwashing by some observers. The term brings to mind images of torture, mysterious methods of controlling thought, and psychological manipulation. Although there is little evidence to suggest anything quite so cabalistic in the thought reform process, there is no doubt that the rise of a new, pervasive, and eminently confident Maoist world view was a shattering experience for the uninitiated. Many Chinese intellectuals were characterized, at the time of the Maoist victory, by confusion, crises of identity, and insecurity. They were unclear about their own loyalties.[6] Confronted with the compelling ideology of Mao some of these intellectuals committed suicide or fled to Hong Kong. It was not a pleasant period for many persons who were unprepared for the revolutionary change.

In 1951 and 1952 there was a program to "liquidate enemy ideology."[7] This was a period of national insecurity; soldiers from China and the United States were fighting each other in Korea. Naturally there was anti-American feeling. Some of this feeling focused on university professors who "worshipped" the American way of doing things.[8] Hostility toward the United States and American imperialism functioned to break the apathy and dependent mentality of some scholars.

In the thought reform process intellectuals were called on to draw "a clear line of demarcation" between self and enemy. Thought reform was also an attempt to overcome selfishness through criticism and self-criticism:

We should not be afraid of criticism and self-criticism, in fear that it may lower our personal prestige. Quite to the contrary, our prestige will suffer increasingly the more we refuse to accept criticism and the more we dislike criticizing ourselves.[9]

Robert Lifton noted that thought reform is seen by the Chinese Communists as a "morally uplifting experience."[10] In small group discussion there is a chance for rehabilitation as people discuss their faults and self-centeredness with others. Sometimes genuine moral conversion takes place. Allyn Rickett, who spent four years in a Chinese prison on spying charges in the early 1950s, gives the following example out of his prison experience.

A new prisoner named Li was placed in the cell with Rickett's group. He had been arrested for supplying information to enemy agents. It turned out that Li had also been a successful pickpocket. On one occasion he was caught with goods stolen from another prisoner. Heated discussion followed:

On we went, trying to make Li think out himself why he was addicted to stealing, but we were able only to scratch the surface. We could go only so far and then Li would say he did not know. We still could not get him to think out why he had become a habitual criminal, how he looked on stealing itself, or what his justifications for it were.

Li was caught stealing again in another cell and made to do a thoroughgoing self-criticism.

Layer after layer of his motivations had gradually come to light, until the heart of the matter had been reached.

Li, as a child, had been abandoned by his parents and picked up by a gang of thieves. At first he was used as a beggar. . . . Later he had been taught the art of a pickpocket. Whatever he got he turned over to the gang. He was virtually their slave, and when he displeased them he was beaten and starved.

He had lived in a realm of fear: fear of his masters, fear of the police, fear of everything around him. . . .

After liberation he had been arrested once as a pickpocket, but had been allowed to go after promising to reform. However, with no conception of how to work for a living, he had quickly drifted back to the only things he knew—stealing, informing, and running away. As his pathetic story had unfolded he had broken into tears and had begun to realize the hopelessness and sordidness of his former life. . . .

His cell mates reasoned with him that there was nothing that did not come about through someone's labor, and that stealing the fruits of another man's work was criminal. . . . They managed to break down Li's fear a little and helped him to come to understand his relationship to society and the wrongness of what he had been doing.

In reasoning with Li it was pointed out that part of the problem was his own selfishness and part was the fault of the old society which created such conditions. Li developed a passionate hatred for the old society and became almost obsessed with the dream of a world in which there would be no fear or want.

The authorities then did a strange thing. This spineless pickpocket, the dregs of humanity, was made leader of a cell. For the first time in his life he was given some responsibility and a position of respect. In coming to a realization of his own background he found that he could help others and in so doing help himself. His fears gradually disappeared almost completely.

I hardly recognized Li the next time I saw him, almost two years later, when we were exercising in the same compound. He seemed inches taller and when he looked at you it was straight in the eye. There was not a shadow of his former cringing self. I heard that he had joined the prison literacy classes and applied himself so well that he could now read and write. Just before I was released I read in the prison newspaper that he had been given an award for the proposal he had made for increasing production in the prison sock factory. I had no doubt that he was well on his way toward building a new life and would soon be released.[11]

Such experiences do not change the fact that intellectuals very often found thought reform to be an excruciating experience and were sometimes mistreated. Mao, reflecting back in 1957, admitted that some intellectuals had been treated unfairly in the transitional period. He played down the harshness of the experience, however, by saying that some communist leaders had been too "crude" and "disrespectful" in dealing with intellectuals. Thought reform, he said, had been carried out in the past "in a somewhat rough and ready fashion," and "the feelings of some people had been hurt."[12] An experience that drove some people to suicide and others to flee the country had been more severe than Mao's words would suggest.

As with landlord executions, severe treatment of intellectuals at the hands of some officials during the transitional period was an example of revolutionary terror and gave rise to an extremely critical evaluation of the new regime by outside observers. The mistakes may not have been as gentle as official pronouncements would have us believe, but neither is it likely that things were as bad as some of the worst horror stories repeated in the West would have it.

By 1957 the situation was more secure and Mao could say that those intellectuals who did not accept Marxist ideas but were law-abiding should be given suitable jobs and let alone. On the other hand, this compromise with old thinking did not mean that those committed to liberation should think there was "no longer any reason to concern oneself with . . . the future of the motherland or the ideals of mankind." Self-revolutionization and the building of a new socialist society was a continuing task even if there were some who could not liberate their thought enough to enter the process positively.

Was thought reform dehumanizing? Did it mean thought control and psychological manipulation? For some, in the transitional period, this may have seemed the case. The struggle did go to extremes. Brainwashing, however, is not a term that is used by many observers of China today. China has not discovered some secret method of making everyone conform to a set of ideas. The variety of viewpoints among emigrants from China attests to this. The basic method of thought reform (criticism and self-criticism in small groups) is used not only in dealing with deviant behavior, but is a process of growth and personal development used throughout Chinese society. The abuses of thought reform in the transitional period do not negate its positive potential.[13] In the attempt to create a nonexploitative society transformation of individual identity is crucial.

Transformation of identity. Intellectuals were not seen as enemies in the same sense that capitalists and landowners were. They were not workers or peasants, however, and were considered to be living off the labor of others. In 1949, intellectuals made up less than 1 percent of the population, but they constituted a major problem for the new regime, which inherited the whole educational system of the earlier society. (In China, intellectual refers to professional people, artists, teachers, and journalists among others.) The question was how the older intellectuals, and the new scholars who were being trained by them, could become proletarian intellectuals. How is it possible to train scholars who will not see their education as a means of obtaining special privilege and prestige? Can intellectuals be trained who identify with the common people, who are prepared to do physical labor, who do not see themselves as superior to manual workers? Such scholars would have to depart from the traditional Chinese understanding that those who do mental labor rule and that those who do physical labor are ruled.

As with landowners and capitalists, so also with intellectuals, the Maoists are optimistic. They recognize that the task of creating "working class intellectuals" is difficult, but they seem to be convinced that it is possible. Western scholars often see the Chinese approach as anti-intellectual. This judgment may simply reflect the unconscious realization that if China can develop a system in which scholars and laborers live on the same level it may threaten the deference given to scholarly position in the West. The Maoist attitude is "prointellectual" in that it is hopeful about the possibility of petty-bourgeois intellectuals being transformed and becoming part of the people of the new socialist society.

How is this transformation of identity possible? Franz Schurmann has pointed out that Marxism is seen in China as a world view which is appropriated by particular individuals and not by classes. One's thought is conditioned by one's social situation but not completely determined by it. The transformation of class stand is possible for anyone, regardless of class origin, who can combine correct theory with correct practice.[14]

Schurmann noted that the mind of an individual is an arena in which class struggle takes place in the process of thought reform. He said that the process was called *fanshen* (literally "turning the body round"), which Schurmann renders as "transformation of identity."[15] In fact the term *fanshen* had a more limited usage in China and generally referred to the peasants' change from an attitude of subservience to one of confidence and opposition to the powerful landlords.[16] The term "self-revolutionization" has been used more extensively in China and better describes the process of transformation.

According to Schurmann, Mao's thought includes both a rationality and a moral force. The rationality is European (Marxist) in origin. The moral force is derived from the Taoist idea of the "Mandate of Heaven," which has often been associated with rebellion in Chinese history. In addition to a rational appeal, thought reform also includes "moral and emotional appeals" that are major factors in the transformation process.[17] This transformation is not a once-and-for-all experience; since thought can change and evolve, the process is never-ending.[18]

There is a danger of misinterpreting the Maoist position if

the question of personal conversion loses its class context. Although it is true that Marxism is appropriated by individuals, this is not simply a process of accepting a set of ideas that have a rational and moral appeal. Transformation of identity means a change of class stand. This requires difficult continuous struggle.

Class stand. The question of identity relates to how one views oneself in relation to nation, culture, work, world view, and class. To be an intellectual is part of one's self-identity. What it means to be a writer, scholar, artist is influenced by cultural and class concepts. Prior to the revolution intellectual pursuits followed either the old "feudal" patterns or new bourgeois patterns. How can one adopt proletarian or socialist or revolutionary styles of intellectual activity after the victory of the revolution? It requires a reinterpretation of what learning is all about. Many assumptions have to be investigated, criticized, and changed.

For example, one assumption was that there are common human feelings that are not influenced by class. On this basis some scholars argue that all persons appreciate the beauty of nature and all are involved in a common effort to obtain the necessities of life and to achieve personal development. The Maoists reject this view and say that class influences are not absent from these concerns. A "starved and sweating" worker has no time to appreciate nature. An exploiter seeks "personal development" by utilizing other people. The oppressed will view these issues differently from oppressors. To be transformed means standing with the oppressed in analyzing questions such as beauty and personal fulfillment.[19]

Another assumption was that literature could serve the socialist cause by arousing the conscience of the enemy class through an appeal to common human feelings. The Maoists also reject this approach, calling it naive and utopian. Although there might be occasional instances of people changing on the basis of such appeals, the structures of wealth and power cannot be changed except by revolutionary struggle. When the power of the enemy class is broken, then the conditions are created for the possible transformation of their thought.[20]

Maoist faith in the efficacy of thought reform does not mean that society can be revolutionized through a series of personal conversions without power struggle. There is a tendency for the intellectual, influenced by bourgeois values, to assume too much about the power of literature and persuasion.

A change of class stand means joining in the struggle against oppression and seeing the world from the perspective of the victims of exploitation. Personal fulfillment is found in the struggle for justice. Obtaining the necessities of life is to be a communal and not an individual concern. The issue of power, how it is used, and by whom it is wielded, cannot be separated from scholarly concerns. Taking this approach to power questions, intellectuals can be transformed and join with the common people, but it is not an easy change.

Party functionaries frequently had a difficult time following the Maoist theory. There have been stories over the years of unfair prejudice against children of former landlords and capitalists. One young man, for example, was the son of a "hated despotic landlord." His father was executed in 1951. The son accepted this "righteous judgment of the people," and supported the new regime. He became an active member of the Youth League. Later, however, he was criticized for sending money to his widowed mother. This criticism was eventually recognized as unfair and not in accordance with Party policy.[21]

In another case a young person wrote to a newspaper to enquire whether one would lose one's "stand" by marrying a person from a formerly exploiting family. The answer given by the paper was no, as long as the person had reformed. A person must be judged according to his or her behavior.[22] The very fact that the question had to be asked indicates continuing prejudice.

It is necessary to reiterate again and again that class background does not decide everything. People from ruling-class background can become revolutionaries if they have a high degree of revolutionary consciousness, exert effort to remold themselves, and follow the Party's advice. Persons from feudal families had given their lives for the revolution.[23] One cannot choose one's family background, but a person can decide his or her own political conviction.[24] When a person from an exploiting class background "takes the road of revolution" his or her old class thought disappears gradually through a long process of reform.[25] This process of transformation and re-education continues to the present day.

Continuing re-education. Some people, Maoists included, may have thought that in five or ten years, or at least in a generation, the problem of intellectuals would have been solved. On the other hand, a careful reading of Mao's theory of continuing contradictions suggests that the struggle will go on for some time. Since selfishness is not overcome in a generation, the continued selfish misuse of education for personal gain or position is not surprising.

The task the Maoists have taken on in transforming intellectuals is a formidable one. It requires the development of a new-style proletarian intellectual and the revamping of the entire educational system. The task is far from complete and some may doubt that it can be accomplished. What is being sought is an educational system and a pattern of scholarly life that is different from any earlier mode. For the Maoists the question is how to keep education from leading to the rise of a new privileged elite. Education, technology, art, literature, all culture, it is felt, should be for all the people, and not for an in-group, although not everyone can receive the same amount of training. It is necessary to train intellectuals in such a way that they see their acquisition of new skills as a means of serving the people better.

During the early years of the new government, "people's universities" and other educational innovations were tried. By the time of the Cultural Revolution, however, old patterns had again asserted themselves. Students in the "best" schools came predominantly from urban, former middle-class families, or the families of high-ranking government and Party officials. A renewed effort was made in the Cultural Revolution to get at the basic personal and systemic causes of this pervasive pattern. Recruitment procedures were altered to favor ordinary workers and peasants. This is not enough, however, if students selected from these backgrounds simply adopt bourgeois attitudes when they enter school. A new effort is being made to combine work and study and to increase the fluidity of worker and student relationships.

The re-education process attempts to deal with superior attitudes that continue to emerge. Intellectuals, it is said, have to become aware of how they have lived off the labor of the workers and have to begin "to live on their own labor." In this long and arduous process they will learn to overcome their contempt for manual labor and their lack of respect for workers and peasants. Individualism and resentment against collective life will also change. Through study and struggle and work they will be able to "shake off the yoke" of old decadent thought and become bold and innovative.[26]

Self-centeredness is a recalcitrant foe. Two decades after liberation one writer spoke of the need to use Mao's thought in order "to cut out one's selfish heart," and the need to "fight to the end" with enemies in one's thinking.[27] Student Red Guards talked of the struggle against "self" or "egoism" *(si)*. They said:

We must make revolution in the depths of our souls, launch vigorous ideological [thought] struggle and serious criticism and self-criticism to defeat "egoism." . . . In transforming the objective world we must, at the same time, transform our inner, subjective world.[28]

Such transformation requires that university students and graduates be re-educated by the workers and peasants in order to develop a proletarian world outlook. The fact that this is necessary a generation after the communist revolution shows that earlier reforms had not prevented traditional attitudes from re-emerging.

Another indication of the persistence of traditional ideas is the ongoing campaign against Confucian elitism. Decades of reform have not broken the hold of Confucian values on the minds of many Chinese. If the attempt to create a new kind of intellectual seems radical from a Western point of view, it is all the more radical given the Confucian background of China.

The Maoists see in the Confucian tradition certain themes that are opposed to their image of the new-style working class intellectual. Confucianism is criticized for encouraging students to seek fame and fortune and making them look down on physical labor and on those who work with their hands. The Confucian view took administrative and scholarly work as superior. The object of study was to escape from physical work into the more privileged realm of the educated elite. Class struggle in the educational field and particularly the reforms since the Cultural Revolution are directed against such values. The object of education should be to train young people to be workers who have a socialist consciousness.[29]

Evaluation. We have dealt with the question of transforming those who fall outside the revolutionary circle—enemies, landlords, capitalists, bourgeois and Confucian intellectuals. In the following section we will consider the continuing transformation of the revolutionaries and proletarians and Party members themselves. The two groups are not entirely distinct, since the need for self-revolutionization among the proletariat and Party members results from the continuing influence of feudal or bourgeois thinking.

The treatment of enemies and intellectuals during the transition period was seen to have been marred by terror tactics. Executions were extensive and thought reform techniques shattered the lives of some people. Mao himself admitted that errors were made. There is also evidence from this same period that not all penal thought reform went to extremes, and that there were positive results in rehabilitation.

Thought reform is a process that gives those from an exploiting class background the possibility of entering the new proletarianized society as creative participants. After the revolution, capitalists, landlords, and bourgeois intellectuals had the opportunity of changing their class stand. They did not have the choice of continuing to live off the labor of others. If they were willing to do physical labor and stand on the side of the peasants and workers, they could contribute to the development of a new China.

Several decades of socialist practice have not eliminated the traditional tendencies of denigrating workers and of using education as a means of personal advancement. Continuing re-education is still necessary to overcome the attitudes of superiority, elitism, and selfishness, which the Maoists feel characterize Confucian and bourgeois mentalities. Old ideas are deeply ingrained, and even the coming of age of a generation reared totally under communist rule has not ended the struggle.

Several questions confront us as we look at this process of transforming enemies and intellectuals in China. Is the goal humane? Is the procedure humane? Is the goal realistic?

Is the goal humane? The object of the transformation process is to rehabilitate those who had lived off the labor of others so that they can be reintegrated into the new society. This new society is to be a community of cultured workers; all persons work and all have access to the cultural and other resources of the nation. It is to be a society without a privileged elite who see themselves as superior to ordinary workers and peasants. No matter how we feel about the Maoist goal it would be difficult to characterize it as inhumane.

Is the procedure humane? The terror of the early years was obviously not humane, but in the broad sweep of the revolution this terror may not have been avoidable. The basic method of transformation was through a process of criticism and self-criticism. As with group therapy sessions in the West, this can often be painful. It requires digging into one's personality to see what one's motivations and values are.

In this self-criticism the question is asked: For whom do I do what I do? Whom do I serve, self or others? In dealing with artists and writers Mao raised this question of "for whom." An artist, he said, can decide "to take the class stand of the proletariat." Mao contrasted Lu Xun, a writer who served the cause of the proletarian revolution, with Zhou Zuoren, who served the imperialists. Lu Xun and Zhou Zuoren were, in fact, brothers, yet Mao said they belonged to different classes because of the stands they took and the people they served.[30]

This way of posing the moral question can be very agonizing. There is no middle ground of academic neutrality. Either one serves the oppressors or one serves those who are struggling for liberation. To serve the oppressed means siding with the people "in deed as well as in word."[31]

For persons who have always worked or studied in order "to get ahead" there may be pain and agony in the self-critical reappraisal of one's motivations. This does not mean that the process is inhumane.

Is the goal of transformation a realistic one? This question has to be considered on several levels. If by realistic it is meant that the goal is achievable in the foreseeable future, then the answer is no. The final transformation of all persons into unselfish servants of the people does not seem to be possible, on the basis of present evidence. On the basis of Mao's own philosophy of eternal contradictions, it would also seem that such an achievement is not possible. As long as history continues there will be contradiction and struggle in people's thought.

If by realistic is meant that progress in transformation can be made, then the answer would be a qualified yes. The re-education of intellectuals to the point where they are willing to look at things from a communal rather than a self-centered view, and where they are willing to combine mental and manual labor, seems to have been partially achieved. Teachers and Party officials participate regularly in physical labor. To some extent there has been a break in the distinction between intellectual and worker, administrator and rank and file, the expert and the peasant, the cultured elite and the masses, the artist and ordinary folk.

The answer is qualified, however, since the continuing reforms of the Cultural Revolution and the anti-Confucian campaign indicate failure up to this point in establishing a new model of trained experts. Progress has been made but the struggle continues.

The fact that campaigns and struggle go on indicates that the Chinese leaders realize that the goal has not been achieved completely. This is healthier than assuming that the transformation has been total and that therefore no more effort is necessary.

A factor that should be borne in mind when considering the

transformation of enemies and intellectuals is that this process does not assume that revolutionaries and proletarians are themselves without need of transformation. The re-education of landlords and scholars through criticism and self-criticism is an extension to those groups of a method of personal development to which the revolutionaries also subject themselves.

The Personal Transformation of Revolutionaries

Maoists see revolution as both a social and personal struggle. The overthrow of exploitative social structures has to be accompanied by a painstaking effort to change the thought patterns that support those structures. Revolution in thought is necessary not only for the exploiters but for the workers and peasants as well.

Contradictions characterize every phenomenon, including the Communist Party and the mind of the most ardent revolutionary. This means that constant thought struggle must take place in order to progress and to avoid regression. Revolutionaries should recognize that their thinking can be infected by nonproletarian ideas. Thought struggle and study can help them to overcome erroneous tendencies and to consolidate a proletarian world view. They must avoid the rut of following orders without question. Since the Party is characterized by contradiction it will not always be right.

They must also avoid regression in their thought. If they are successful in some task they may become arrogant; if they fail they may become anxious. Both errors can be avoided only by a constant process of criticism and self-criticism and an unceasing effort to reform their thought.[32]

In the transformation of revolutionaries the following points need attention: Self-revolutionization is a permanent process; bourgeois temptations are always present, necessitating class struggle in the mind of the revolutionary; no one is automatically red or a flawless revolutionary; revisionism is a new bourgeois tendency that is even more dangerous because it comes in the guise of Marxism.

Self-revolutionization. The concept of self-revolutionization has already been referred to in the discussion of the transformation of intellectuals. It is also a key concept for understanding the approach of Maoists to the self-development of revolutionaries. It was said during the Cultural Revolution that revolutionaries must take themselves as targets of revolution. Carrying out progressive action was not only a matter of fighting exploitation but also of struggling against exploitative tendencies within oneself.

This understanding of the person involved in the struggle for social justice has many significant implications. It means that the struggle is not only against an objective enemy but against a subjective one as well. Implied here is the need for a deep, personal, ongoing process of conversion. Mao's philosophy at this point has some resemblance to a religious view of the meaning of personal development. It is necessary to make revolution to the depths of one's soul.

Self-revolutionization is the struggle of the soul, and like the social revolution of which it is a part, it is a never-ending process. The ceaseless struggle of opposing forces, both objective and subjective, social and personal, propels life forward. If there were no thought struggle life itself would end.[33] In the lifelong process of self-revolutionization a person seeks to adhere to the proletarian stand, identify with workers and peasants, and serve the people. This means making every effort to destroy one's selfish thought and to establish proletarian thought. The struggle "knows no end" because there is always a higher degree of consciousness that one can achieve and greater contributions that one can make.[34]

Maoists place heavy emphasis on this revolution of thought within the total revolutionary process. Although it is Marxist theory that the economic system, the ownership of the means of production, the social situation, give rise to thought and culture, nevertheless, say the Maoists, thought plays a "tremendous and dynamic role." Under certain conditions thought plays "a decisive role" in the development of the politics and economics of a society. Old-style thinking hinders progress. Revolutionary ideas can be grasped by the people and turned into "a powerful material force which promotes social progress."[35] Mao says that this view of the influence of thought on the economic base is consistent with Marxist materialism:

Are we going against materialism when we say this? No. The reason is that while we recognize that in the general development of history the material determines the mental, and social being determines social consciousness, we also—and indeed must— recognize the reaction of the mental on material things, of social consciousness on social being, and of the superstructure on the economic base. This does not go against materialism; on the contrary it avoids mechanical materialism and firmly upholds dialectical materialism.[36]

The significance of one's thinking, and the tempering which comes through self-revolutionization, has deep roots in Mao's philosophy and in his own experience. The following passage from his writing is an example:

If you want the masses to understand you, if you want to be one with the masses, you must make up your mind to undergo a long and even painful process of tempering. Here I might mention the experience of how my own feelings changed. I began life as a student and at school acquired the ways of a student; I then used to feel it undignified to do even a little manual labour, such as carrying my own luggage in the presence of my fellow students, who were incapable of carrying anything, either on their shoulders or in their hands. At that time I felt that intellectuals were the only clean people in the world, while in comparison workers and peasants were dirty. I did not mind wearing the clothes of other intellectuals, believing them clean, but would not put on clothes belonging to a worker or peasant, believing them dirty. But after I became a revolutionary and lived with workers and peasants and with soldiers of the revolutionary army, I gradually came to know them well, and they gradually came to know me well too. It was then, and only then, that I fundamentally changed the bourgeois and petty-bourgeois feeling implanted in me in the bourgeois schools. I came to feel that compared with the workers and peasants the unremolded intellectuals were not clean, and that in the last analysis, the workers and peasants were the cleanest people and even though their hands were soiled and their feet smeared with cow-dung, they were really cleaner than the bourgeois and petty-bourgeois intellectuals. That is what is meant by a change in feelings, a change from one class to another.[37]

In this passage Mao expressed the need for the would-be revolutionary to get rid of bourgeois and petty-bourgeois feelings. The problem of bourgeois temptations in the path of one's revolutionary development has been a recurring theme in Maoist writings.

The bourgeois temptations. Self-revolutionization means making every effort to overcome the bourgeois world outlook. This outlook is characterized by selfishness, individualism, and other egocentric attitudes. The revolutionary leader is always in danger of feeling self-important. This will only separate him from the people. In addition, living in a country where the liberation struggle has been successful may lead a person to covet a life of ease, luxury, and wastefulness.[38]

To be a revolutionary in peace times is in some ways more difficult than armed struggle. A person "brought up in a peaceful environment that knows only songs but not gunfire" is easily subject to bourgeois corrosion.[39] Those who are against socialism may use "sugar-coated bullets" to tempt the revolutionaries into selfishness and to corrupt their dedication to the common good.[40]

Even if no one is trying to corrupt the revolutionaries they must still persevere in the struggle to transform their souls. The "insidious invasion of bourgeois ideology" or the "influence of old thinking, old customs, old culture, and old habits" can be a problem no matter how dedicated one is.

The struggle against bourgeois thinking is not only a struggle against the former ruling class. It is also a struggle against selfish modes of thought that distort the work style and attitudes of the proletarian revolutionary. Recognition by the Maoists that self-revolutionization and struggle against bourgeois selfishness is needed also by themselves is recognition that no one is a flawless revolutionary.

No flawless revolutionaries. In the Maoist view there is no room for arrogance on the part of those who are on the side of the revolution. No one, Party member, worker, peasant, liberation fighter, child of a revolutionary martyr, is "automatically red." No one is without flaws.

It is an error to assume that someone from the "right kind of family" is automatically revolutionary. In Chinese parlance, the right kind of family means worker, peasant, or liberation soldier background. Proletarian children are not red by birth. They must still "exert the utmost effort in remolding and improving" their thought.

Lei Feng, for example, came from humble origins. The suffering he endured had an important influence on his development. Nevertheless, say the Maoists, he still needed thought struggle. Through subjective effort he was able to change his personal hatred for the landlord who had wronged him and his family into class hatred. He was able, that is, to move from a simple desire for revenge to a concern for the poor of the world who are still suffering oppression, and to dedicate "all his energies and his whole life to communism—the cause of the liberation of all mankind."[41] This was possible for Lei Feng, it is said, because he practiced self-criticism and did not take himself as a flawless revolutionary.

It is pointed out that deciding to fight for the revolution is easier than struggling against one's own flaws and errors. It is necessary not only to see oneself as an integral part of the revolutionary force, but also to go on to the difficult task of seeing one's own need for continuing self-revolutionization:

It is certainly an agonizing thing to regard oneself as a target of revolution. There is an unceasing violent struggle in one's mind between community interest and selfishness, and between proletarian thinking and bourgeois thinking. But genuine revolutionaries deeply understand that to revolutionize themselves is by no means an extra burden but is intended to emancipate themselves thoroughly from the sludge and foul water of the old world. Therefore, genuine revolutionaries surely fear no pain and no disgrace in revolutionizing themselves, but will vigorously rebel to the end against selfishness.[42]

A revolutionary needs to be brave enough "to touch his own soul," to see the "opposites in his mind," and to advance by overcoming them. This struggle will continue because contradictions "exist universally and forever." The "changes and movement of the objective realistic world are endless," and the "apprehension of truth through practice will also never end."[43] It is said that:

There will still be contradictions after a thousand or ten thousand or even a hundred million years. Contradictions will exist in the universe even after the destruction of the earth and the extinction of the sun. All things are in a flux of contradiction, struggle, and change. This is the Marxist-Leninist outlook. The essence of Marxism is critical and revolutionary. Its basic spirit is criticism, struggle and revolution. This alone can propel our socialist cause forward.[44]

Revolutionaries, then, must always engage in thought struggle, must constantly reaffirm the decision of what kind of persons they want to be,[45] and must put this into practice in their lives with the people. Leaders must engage in physical labor on farms and in factories in order to get rid of "bureaucratic airs." There should be criticism, debates, use of wall posters, and mass meetings, in order to involve all the people in this transformation.[46] Thought struggle is intensely personal, but it can develop only in a communal setting.

Revisionism. A Chinese slogan particularly prominent during the Cultural Revolution was "fight self and repudiate revisionism" *(dousi pixiu).* Slogans like these are moral axioms, not dissimilar in form to traditional ethical teachings in China, although the content is different. The first half of the slogan, fight self, has to do with the whole effort we have been describing, to rid one's thought of self-centeredness.

The second half of the slogan, repudiate revisionism, has to do with the particular problem of the corruption of revolutionary Marxism by those who seek to create a new privileged elite. Revisionism represents a new class, those "persons in authority taking the capitalist road." These persons are "infected" with the thinking of the exploiting classes inherited from earlier generations. Selfishness, it is said, still has a tenacious hold on their thinking, and they have not transformed their souls.[47] Within the working class, revisionism appears as a new version, in revolutionary garb, of the old system of capitalist selfishness. To repudiate revisionism requires combating both self-interest and new social structures that are based on such self-interest.[48]

The fact that revisionism could arise among the working class and Marxist leaders themselves indicates the need to continue to struggle. Lin Biao,[49] who has been criticized in the anti-Confucian campaign, is accused of having said that struggle causes enmity. The Maoist position is that enmity is caused by class antagonism, and that revisionism is one source of such antagonism. Calling for harmony will not overcome animosity. Struggle, criticism, self-criticism, and the correction of errors are necessary if unity is to be achieved.[50]

To sum up. We have been looking at the process of personal transformation of revolutionaries. The problems and processes are similar to those involved in the transformation of non-revolutionaries—enemies and bourgeois intellectuals. Personal transformation is linked with social transformation. Self-revolutionization is an integral part of the whole process of social revolution. The basic egocentricism of the thought of those living in the prerevolutionary system continues as a problem for revolutionaries themselves. Bourgeois, feudal, and Confucian thought patterns still plague the working class, Marxist leaders, and the most ardent revolutionaries.

Humility rather than arrogance, self-criticism rather than complacency are necessary. People cannot sit back and say that since they are workers, or Party members, or soldiers, they therefore have made a complete and final break with selfishness.

In each new situation that arises the unending process of thought struggle must continue for the revolutionary. One can never adopt a casual or leisurely attitude towards this struggle, but must have the revolutionary spirit of "seizing the day and seizing the hour." The revolutionization of one's thought is not "accomplished at a stroke." Further progress or regress is always possible.[51]

Evaluation

This chapter has dealt with the question of personal transformation, both of nonrevolutionaries and of revolutionaries. On the transformation of enemies and intellectuals the point was made that although there were some extremes and abuses during the transitional period, in the longer sweep of the

Chinese revolution the attempt to reform these persons has not been inhumane in theory or practice. In fact, this reform is based on the optimistic view that people from exploiting-class backgrounds can transform themselves into productive members of the new society. Some significant achievements are being made in this regard.

The transformation of nonrevolutionaries is accomplished by the same methods that Maoists use to revolutionize their own thinking. It is not assumed that proletarians and Marxists are without fault and in no need of change. A long and painful process of thought struggle is necessary for everyone in the society.

The life and work of each person, regardless of class background, is judged by the question "For whom?" Is what one does for the sake of selfish motives or for the common good? Is it for self or for others? This is the kind of question that cannot be answered for oneself in isolation. In small group meetings of criticism and self-criticism the issues are raised. Answers are not only in terms of words but also of actions. One must join selflessly in the work and life and hardships of the peasants and workers.

The struggle against arrogance, selfishness, elitism, authoritarianism, discouragement, lack of confidence, and all forms of egocentrism is one that goes on at the very depths of one's soul, the Maoists say. This point seems to be missed by Lucien Pye in his analysis of the concept of "sin" in contemporary China.[52] Pye suggests that the Russian Communists, because of their heritage of the Christian doctrine of original sin, are more aware than the Chinese of the need "to grapple with the inner weakness of the soul" and "to be constantly on guard against the triumph of evil." The Chinese do not have this sense of sin, writes Pye:

In the Chinese view, as well articulated in the Confucian as in the Communist traditions, man—that is, Chinese man—is inherently good, and all he needs is education, training, or discipline to bring out his basic goodness.

The Russians recognize the need to overcome laziness, emotionalism, and other personal weaknesses, which means a "physically exhausting struggle at the very roots of the personality." For the Chinese, according to Pye, the process of becoming a good Communist, although sometimes "painful," is a simpler matter of pragmatic re-education rather than personality change.

This interpretation by Pye of the Maoist view of personality change is wide of the mark. There seems to be ample evidence that the Maoists see the need for a deep and continuous process of personality development.

Is it true that in Mao's view human beings are basically good? This is only one side of Mao's complex understanding of human life. Selfishness is seen as part of the class nature of society inherited from generation to generation. In addition, however, Mao's theory of contradiction would suggest that the struggle that goes on in the mind of the individual is one form of conflict that is part of the very nature of the universe, society, and subjective thought. The contradictions in thought will not be finally overcome by any simple process of training, but will require a lifelong struggle.

Though Mao's philosophy has analogies with religion, it is distinguished from many religious world views in that the struggle of the soul is seen as *class* struggle. Enemy thought is to be destroyed by education, thought struggle, criticism, and self-criticism—which continue after the revolution as nonantagonistic struggle among the people. Although this self-revolutionization may reach "to the depths of one's soul," it is not an individualistic process that can be carried out in monastic solitude "behind closed doors." It is class struggle that takes place in a social context, and not an internalized experience of overcoming sin and self through individual faith or meditation.

A dimension of Mao's thought that does border on a religious world view is his apparently paradoxical understanding of struggle. If selfishness is a historical phenomenon that arose with the rise of classes, then through struggle it should eventually be overcome completely. If it is the result of an eternal process of contradiction, then there is no way it can be completely overcome. There is here both the question of the source of sin and selfishness—whether historical in origin or a natural phenomenon—and the question of what is possible for human beings to achieve in history. At the very heart of Mao's thought is a seeming paradox, since it is both affirmed that it will be possible to end the exploitation of person by person, and it is also affirmed that contradiction and revolutionary struggle are permanent and eternal. The significance of this paradox will be discussed in our final chapter.

One final area to consider in this evaluation is the conflict between Chinese thought reform and Western liberal values in general. This will only be touched on here since the question of liberalism and liberal values will be covered in chapter 5.

The Chinese system of thought reform is open to the possible distortion that any dissent will be labeled bourgeois or revisionist by persons in authority who do not want to be criticized. The Cultural Revolution revealed that there had been numerous instances of such tactics. Westerners might feel that if there were open scholarly dissent, opposition journalism, and a pluralistic system this misuse of power could be avoided.

For the Maoist these liberal values are seen from the point of view of class struggle. They feel that in the West the media and educational institutions are controlled by the upper classes and do not, in fact, give workers and the poor equal freedom of expression with the rich. The Maoists fear that to reintroduce liberal values into China would simply give rise to the inequalities and exploitative practices of capitalist societies.

It is a false delineation of the problem to contrast Western freedom with Chinese thought control. There are problems on both sides. The Chinese may be too conformist, and the words they use to express themselves may sound too much like jargon. There is room for dissent, however, through wall posters, criticism sessions, debates. The problem the Chinese are trying to solve is how to have dissent and independence of thought without opening the door to selfish individualism.

We in the West might well ask ourselves how academic freedom and free expression in our society relate to economic privilege. Do minorities, the rural poor, workers, have equal access to free expression through the established media? Another question is what our freedom is used for. Is it used as a means of serving others or serving self?

Neither the liberal West nor Maoist China has so far been able to create a situation where freedom of expression leads to a spirit of service and identification with the least well off members of society. In denying that persons should be free to amass huge fortunes and to exploit others, the Maoists may deny the kind of free expression we cherish. Affirming such freedom in the West may support the grinding poverty and destruction of community and environment which, on the basis of stated liberal values, we should deplore.

Both Maoism and liberalism profess a commitment to creating a society in which all people have freedom, dignity, and equal access to the resources of the community. The Maoists say that this can be accomplished only by struggle, discipline, personal transformation, and overcoming selfishness. Although it is not possible to make a final judgment about the Maoist approach, I can see little ground on which one could claim that the liberal approach is superior.

NOTES

1. See "Letter to Yang Shih-te," (A.D. 1517), in *The Philosophical Letters of Wang Yang-ming*, trans. and annotated by Julia Ching (Canberra: Australia National University Press, 1972), p. 45. Ching's translation varies from that used here.

2. SW III, p. 235.

3. For a good brief description of thought reform see Victor H. Li, "Introduction," in Allyn and Adele Rickett, *Prisoners of Liberation: Four Years in a Chinese Communist Prison* (New York: Anchor Books, 1973), pp. vi–xv. The book was originally published in 1957 without Li's introduction.

4. SW IV, p. 185.

5. SW IV, p. 186.

6. A major study of thought reform by an outside observer is Robert Jay Lifton, *Thought Reform and the Psychology of Totalism* (London: Victor Gollancz, 1962). His case studies document the insecure position of many Chinese intellectuals at this time. The Ricketts' book *(Prisoners of Liberation)* is a useful description of penal thought reform written by two Americans who spent four years in a Chinese jail in the 1950s. It includes a number of valuable accounts of the experiences of some of their prison mates.

7. Ch'ien Chun-jui, "The Problem of Ideological Reform," *Ta Kung Pao* (Shanghai), November 13, 1951, CB, no. 169 (April 2, 1952), pp. 12–13.

8. Editorial, "Seriously Develop Ideological Reform of College Teachers," *Nan-fang Jih-Pao (Southern Daily)*, May 26, 1952, CB, no. 213 (October 1, 1952), p. 5.

9. Ch'ien Chun-jui, "The Problem of Ideological Reform," *Ta Kung Pao* (Shanghai), November 13, 1951, CB, no. 169 (April 2, 1952), pp. 12–13.

10. Lifton, *Thought Reform*, p. 15.

11. Rickett, *Prisoners of Liberation*, pp. 219–23.

12. FEP, pp. 108–10.

13. Ann Tompkins, *Self-Criticism* (San Francisco: Moon Press, forthcoming).

14. Franz Schurmann, *Ideology and Organization in Communist China* (Berkeley: University of California Press, 1966), pp. 30–31. Schurmann notes that none of the leading figures in Chinese Communism came from proletarian origins.

15. Ibid., p. 32.

16. William Hinton, *Fanshen: A Documentary of Revolution in a Chinese Village* (New York: Monthly Review Press, 1966), p. vii.

17. Schurmann, *Ideology and Organization*, p. 50.

18. Ibid., pp. 32–33.

19. Kuan Feng, "On Human Nature and Class Nature," *Hsueh-hsi (Study)*, no. 17 (September 3, 1957), ECMM, no. 112 (December 23, 1957), pp. 8–17. Kuan Feng was criticized in the Cultural Revolution.

20. Ibid.

21. Chao Sheng-hui, "How Shall We Treat Parents and Relatives Who Are Landlords and Counter-revolutionaries," CY, no. 24 (December 16, 1956), ECMM, no. 65 (January 14, 1967), pp. 12–16.

22. "Does One Lose One's Stand by Marrying a Person Born of a Family of the Exploiting Class?" *Kung-jen Jih-pao (Workers Daily)*, Peking, May 6, 1965, SCMP, no. 3469 (June 2, 1965), pp. 14–15.

23. "What Should We Do If Our Family Background Is Not Good?" KM, April 7, 1965, SCMP, no. 3448 (May 3, 1965), p. 25.

24. Editorial, PD, April 4, 1965, SCMP, no. 3448 (May 3, 1965), p. 25.

25. Wang Jih-tung, "One's Origin, Environment, and Thought," PD, June 1963, SCMP, no. 3004 (June 21, 1973), pp. 1–5.

26. Cheng Ssu-yuan, "Uninterrupted Revolution Is Necessary for Ideological Remolding," *Cheng-chih Hsueh-hsi* (Political Study), no. 8 (August 1958), ECMM, no. 151 (December 22, 1958), pp. 19–22.

27. Wang Tao-ming, "Transform People's Souls with Mao Tse-tung Thought," PD, October 25, 1966, SCMP, no. 3814 (November 3, 1966), pp. 10–11.

28. Third Headquarters of Peking Red Guards, "Eliminate the 'Ego' and Forge a Great Alliance of the Revolutionary Rebels," RF, no. 3 (February 1, 1967), SCMM, no. 564 (February 20, 1967), pp. 5–6.

29. "On Confucius' Educational Thinking," PD, July 19, 1971, translation in *Ta Kung Pao* Weekly English Supplement, Hong Kong, August 26–September 1, 1971, pp. 6–7. Mao at times has had some good things to say about Confucius. See Mao Tse-tung, "Remarks at the Spring Festival, Summary Record, February 13, 1963," in *Mao Unrehearsed,* ed. Stuart Schram (Harmondsworth: Penguin Books, 1974), p. 208. For further observations on the criticisms of Confucius see Robert P. Kramers, "The Case Against Confucius in Chinese Universities Today," *China Notes* 12, no. 3 (Summer 1974), pp. 25–29.

30. SW III, pp. 77–78.

31. *Quotations from Chairman Mao Tse-Tung* (Peking: Foreign Languages Press, 1966), p. 14.

32. Liu Ch'ung, "Ideological Contradictions within the Party," PD, January 25, 1957, SCMP, no. 1473 (February 19, 1957), pp. 2–5. It is interesting that this article contains some points that were integral to Mao Tse-tung's important speech the following month, "On the Correct Handling of Contradictions among the People," which was not published until June of that year.

33. FEP, p. 32.

34. Sun Yi-ch'ing, "Lay Down the Load, Advance with Light Equipment," CYN, March 28, 1963, SCMP, no. 2968 (April 30, 1963) pp. 11–13.

35. Editorial, "Combat Self-interest and Repudiate Revisionism Is the Basic Policy of the Great Proletarian Cultural Revolution," PD, October 6, 1967, SCMP, no. 4038 (October 10, 1967), pp. 17–19.

36. FEP, pp. 58–59.

37. SW III, p. 73.

38. Sun Yi-ch'ing, "Lay Down the Load, Advance with Light Equipment," CYN, March 28, 1963, SCMP, no. 2968 (April 30, 1963), pp. 11–13.

39. Ibid.

40. Wang Jih-tung, "One's Origin, Environment, and Thought," PD, June 1963, SCMP, no. 3004 (June 21, 1963), pp. 1–5.

41. Ibid.

42. Department of Mao Tse-tung Thought Philosophy and Social Science of the Red Guard Alliance, "The Correct Attitude towards Oneself," PD, March 8, 1967, SCMP, no. 3901 (March 17, 1967), p. 19. In the interest of clarity and accuracy I have made some changes in this translation after comparing it with the original Chinese.

43. Jen Li-hsin, "One Must Divide Oneself into Two," PD, July 19, 1967, SCMP, no. 3988 (July 26, 1967), pp. 7–9.

44. Editorial, "A Great Revolution That Touches People to Their Very Souls," PD, June 2, 1966, translated in *The Great Revolution in China* (Hong Kong: Asia Research Centre, 1967), p. 208.

45. Chiang Ju-wang, "Use the Philosophical Concepts of Chairman Mao to Conduct Battle," KM, September 27, 1970, SCMP, no. 4756 (October 13, 1970), p. 82.

46. Cheng Ssu-yuan "Uninterrupted Revolution Is Necessary for Ideological Remolding," *Cheng-chih Hsueh-hsi (Political Study)*, no. 8 (August 1958), ECMM, no. 151 (December 22, 1958), pp. 19–22.

47. Sun Yi-ch'ing, "Lay Down the Load, Advance with Light Equipment," CYN, March 28, 1963, SCMP, no. 2968 (April 30, 1963), pp. 11–13.

48. Editorial, "Combat Self-interest and Repudiate Revisionism Is the Basic Policy of the Great Proletarian Cultural Revolution," PD, October 6, 1967, SCMP, no. 4038 (October 10, 1967), pp. 17–19.

49. Lin Biao, former defense minister, leader of the Cultural Revolution, and once Mao's "heir apparent," was condemned after his reported assassination attempt against Mao and his subsequent death in an air crash while attempting to flee to Russia in September 1971.

50. Hsin Feng, "The Reactionary Essence of the Fallacy of 'Those Who Struggle against One Another Are Enemies and Those Who Live in Harmony Are Friends' of Lin Piao," PD, February 19, 1974, SPRCP, no 5577 (March 21, 1974), pp. 110–14.

51. Ch'en Tse-ch'ai, "It Is Imperative to Continuously Promote Ideological Revolutionization," PD, October 25, 1969, SCMP, no. 4532 (November 6, 1969), pp. 5–6.

52. Lucien W. Pye, *The Spirit of Chinese Politics* (Cambridge: MIT Press, 1968), pp. 60–61.

CHAPTER 4

A REVOLUTION IN LIFESTYLE

We have considered the struggle ethic in the context of social and personal transformation. What kind of lifestyle does this transformation lead to? How complete has the transformation been? There is a great deal of talk in China about the creation of a new person and a new society. Some significant progress has been made, but the Chinese do not assume that there has been any final or complete transformation. Model heroes, such as Lei Feng, are used for educational purposes, as people to be emulated. China's continuing moral campaigns would not be necessary, obviously, if most people's lives were already patterned after such models. The models do indicate the kind of lifestyle being strived for in China.

Some features of this new lifestyle can be easily appreciated by the Western observer, but others are more difficult to grasp. Hard work, a simple life, and basic honesty may have gone out of style in our own societies, but most of us would respond positively to such values. There are other aspects of Chinese lifestyle that undoubtedly strike us as more harsh: strong anti-individualism and antielitism, positive class hatred, social discipline, anticonsumerism, and anticareerism.

Is the Maoist lifestyle basically a creative and attractive lifestyle, or is it characterized by dull conformity? How does the lifestyle of struggle relate to happiness and the joy of living? What special questions of lifestyle arise for those who are in positions traditionally considered more privileged than physical laborers—artists, writers, administrators, teachers, and "professional" people?

The struggle ethic, as we have seen, has a number of dimensions. In social transformation it means that harmony is not possible unless basic social conflicts are brought to the surface, struggled over, and resolved. Even then, harmony is temporary and unstable because new contradictions continue to arise. In personal transformation the struggle ethic means that there is no resting place where one can say that all subjective contradictions have been overcome. Progress or retrogression of thought are both always possible. In relation to lifestyle, the struggle ethic means that life is to be simple, that hard work is not to be shunned, that happiness is found in working with and on behalf of the common people and in struggling for the benefit of others.

Struggle and contradiction are permanent features of life and society, according to Mao. Under such conditions there is a moral imperative to commit oneself to the people and to oppose the enemies of the people. One should show love for the people and animosity toward the exploiters, kindness in dealing with the oppressed and militancy in dealing with oppressors. This attitude is summed up in a couplet by the twentieth-century Chinese writer, Lu Xun. The lines are quoted by Mao in the concluding section of his "Talks at the Yenan Forum on Literature and Art."

> Fierce-browed, I coolly defy
>   a thousand pointing fingers,
> Head-bowed, like a willing ox
>   I serve the children.

Mao comments that the pointing fingers represent the enemies who must be courageously opposed. The children symbolize the people, who are to be served.[1] The revolutionary lifestyle demands both militancy and humble service.

This lifestyle of service and struggle has its origins in the revolutionary war period. Violent struggle was being waged against military enemies, but at the same time people were called on to exhibit love in their interpersonal relationships:

Whenever there is struggle there is sacrifice, and death is a common occurrence. But we have the interests of the people and the sufferings of the great majority at heart, and when we die for the people it is a worthy death. Nevertheless, we should do our best to avoid unnecessary sacrifices. Our cadres must show concern for every soldier, and all people in the revolutionary ranks must care for each other, must love and help each other.[2]

Since the victory of the revolution the style of struggle and the identity of the enemies have changed, but the need for vigilance continues. The struggle has become a moral battle against corrupting influences that could set back the progress of social and personal transformation. This change in the identity of the enemy means a shifting away from class struggle primarily as a battle against landlords and capitalists to a deeper and more long-range fight against competitiveness, acquisitiveness, consumerism, and egocentrism.

We have discussed the thought struggle that is necessary for every person in the new society. This thought struggle requires a vision of a new unselfish lifestyle. To develop a new lifestyle people have to change many of their customs, habits, and expectations. The training of children and youth is crucial, since the family and educational systems introduce them to the values of the society.

To bring children up in a revolutionary lifestyle requires that adults develop and maintain such a style themselves. A start had been made in the war years when simplicity and community effort were a necessity for survival. In 1949, Mao pointed to the long struggle ahead to transform China and the need to continue the spirit and style that had brought revolutionary victory:

The comrades must be taught to remain modest, prudent, and free from arrogance and rashness in their style of work. The comrades must be taught to preserve the style of plain living and hard struggle. We have the Marxist-Leninist weapon of criticism and self-criticism. . . . We are not only good at destroying the old world, we are also good at building the new. Not only can the Chinese people live without begging alms from the imperialists, they will live a better life than that in the imperialist countries.[3]

There is expressed here a confidence that China can build a better life for its people than that of the imperialist countries. Part of this better life will be the style of modesty, simplicity, and struggle.

Features of the Maoist Lifestyle

Plain living and hard struggle (jianku fendou). This phrase was used in Mao's speech quoted above. Frugality and perseverance were developed during the war years at the blockaded communist base area in Yanan. It was necessary to save every scrap of paper and every grain of rice because of the severe shortages.

Under such circumstances it would have been possible for the army to monopolize available goods, but the revolution depended on the support of the people. Soldiers who were not fighting participated in industrial and agricultural work. They were taught to respect the common people and not abuse their own power. Some of the army rules were "Don't take a single needle or a piece of thread from the masses; Speak politely; Pay fairly for what you buy; Return everything you borrow; Pay for anything you damage; Don't hit or swear at people; Don't damage crops; Don't take liberties with women; Don't ill-treat captives."[4]

Such behavior was new for a Chinese army. Since liberation the tradition of staying close to the common people and living simply is still maintained by the army. They continue to grow most of their own food and make their own uniforms in order not to be a burden to the people.

After liberation one army unit in Shanghai received praise for their exemplary behavior in that formerly notorious city. The "Good Eighth Company" resisted the bourgeois temptations of the big city and helped in its transformation. Rather than lord it over the working people they assisted in common tasks such as collecting garbage and pushing manure carts. They persevered in the spirit of struggle and service even after the war had been won.[5]

Dazhai (Tachai), an agricultural commune in a poor area of Shanxi Province, is also a model of plain living and hard struggle. After the overthrow of the landlords and land reform, Dazhai commune members pioneered in using hard physical labor to transform the land. Under the leadership of Chen Yunggui, an illiterate and landless peasant before the revolution, they organized themselves into a disciplined productive force. Working together and relying only on their own strength and the materials that were at hand, they terraced hillsides, improved irrigation, increased dramatically the amount of arable land, and raised their production of crops beyond any previous level. From a community of less than one hundred persons which could not produce enough to feed itself in 1949, it has expanded to nearly five hundred persons with crop surpluses far beyond their own needs.

Life in Dazhai remains simple. Nevertheless, housing for everyone has been improved and made safe, nursery care and education for children are available for all, health care and other needs are met. People still have to work hard, there are few luxuries, but life is secure and happy.

Dazhai is a model for the whole society. There are those who still seek their own special comforts in China, but by and large a life of plain living and hard struggle is the norm. Make-up, fashionable clothes, luxurious houses, fancy cars, expensive jewelry are simply not part of the scene in China today. A "frontier spirit" prevails, although it is communal and not individualistic.

The style of plain living and hard struggle was evident among the 14,000 Chinese who helped build the Tanzania-Zambia railway in East Africa. The doctors and technicians in the group, as well as the railroad workers, lived in utter simplicity like their African colleagues. The only "luxury" they seemed to allow themselves was Chinese cuisine, but they even grew vegetables and raised chickens around the work sites in order to supply their needs.

There are grounds for assuming that not everyone in China chooses to live plainly and to struggle hard. Campaigns to encourage a simple lifestyle continue to take place. It does seem, however, that a frugal lifestyle is being attempted by large numbers of people. This is the style that is encouraged.

Anti-individualism. In China today individualism is equated with selfishness. Western phrases such as "going it alone," "rugged individualism," and "doing your own thing" are unheard of. People work in collective units, every neighborhood is organized. A community spirit prevails. One does not find in China, for example, aged persons living alone and entirely forgotten by the community. The Chinese aphorism "only sweep the snow in front of your own door" has been replaced by an attitude of putting public interest above private concerns.

In sports and athletics, health and friendship are the primary goals. Athletes may strive to perfect their skills, but "championitis" and the seeking of stardom are frowned upon.

Visitors to China in recent years have been impressed with the vast networks of community air-raid shelters being built under the cities. It is interesting to compare this phenomenon with the rash of shelter building in the United States around 1960. Both the Chinese effort and the United States effort may be equally futile in protecting people from nuclear attack. Be that as it may, the Chinese approach has been entirely communal, whereas in the United States shelter building was done on a private basis by relatively wealthy citizens. In the United States there was a controversy over what to do if others tried to get into one's private shelter, where food and air supplies would be inadequate. It was reported that some Christian ethicists approved the use of violence against neighbors under such circumstances. A Chinese writer commented that this advice showed the depravity of "bourgeois morality."[6] The "depravity" is in the individualistic approach to shelter building, as well as in what is done when the bombs are falling. This individualism contrasts dramatically with the Chinese community spirit and collective style.

Personal struggle against individualism is described by one young factory worker. As a high school student he had read certain books that encouraged self-interest. He began to feel that "a little individualism" did not matter, and set his heart on getting money, a house, and other comforts. The older workers in the automobile factory where he worked criticized his individualistic concern for selfish goals.

Although I did not yield to the criticism, I was distressed in my mind and felt a spiritual void in myself. I saw that the others were quite happy and enthusiastic in their work, but I felt different from them, as though I had left the collective, and I gradually started to envy their happiness.

In this state of distress and "melancholy" the worker was led to read Mao's writings, which "opened his eyes." He realized that individualism had distorted his thinking, and that to be happy he had to overcome selfishness and seek to serve the people:

Now my spiritual condition is different and I constantly remain vigilant about the possible inroads of bourgeois thinking; I constantly fight against my own individualism. In such a fashion I have become contented with my work, my enthusiasm has increased and I no longer plot to get more wages and rewards. I often obtain spiritual happiness in overcoming difficulties and completing assignments.[7]

Does the attitude expressed in this example make Mao's thought an "opiate"? Does it simply lead workers to find spiritual (*jingshenshang*) contentment under poor working conditions, rather than try to improve their lives? Such a criticism would be true only if the workers' enthusiasm was being utilized and manipulated for the benefit of some small group. In a nation where leaders and administrators are also leading simple lives and are participating in the struggle to overcome individualism and special privilege, workers can participate in collective effort without feeling they are exploited. If a new class emerged, living off the efforts of the workers, the whole collective process would be undermined. This is why the "cadre problem," which will be discussed subsequently, is so important.

The spirit of collective effort in Chinese socialism is diametrically opposed to the capitalist spirit of the West. Western capitalism is based on the theory that all persons struggle for their own self-interest in a spirit of competitiveness. This arouses enthusiasm, leads to greater productivity, and results in a better life for all, according to capitalist theory. The Chinese feel that such an individualistic approach is bound to lead to divisiveness, greed, discontent, exploitation, and violent struggle by the exploited against the ruling classes.

During the Cultural Revolution the slogan "all public, no self" was in vogue. This meant one should have only community interest and no personal goals. The late Premier Zhou Enlai (Chou En-lai) criticized this. Public, collective concerns should be put first, but personal interests cannot be eliminated. In an interview Zhou said:

We hold that without individuals there is no collective. *What we advocate is putting the collective first.* . . . We get together but each of us has different thoughts and different words. In the end we may agree on a few basic things and for these goals held in common we should fight together. But as soon as we go into action each will arrive at his or her own personal explanation again, so that our unity is temporary and our differences are protracted. In spite of this we may make agreement on our main direction and set our differences to one side as exceptions, as individual variations. . . .

The bourgeoisie curse us and say we only want the collective and no individual expression, but that is not correct. In fact it is the capitalists who carry the thing to extremes by stressing only the individual and no collective responsibility.[8]

Personal expression has a necessary place, but community concerns are primary in the Chinese system.

Self-reliance. Another feature of the Maoist lifestyle is self-reliance (*zili gengsheng*). This was also a necessary characteristic during the war years when liberation forces were compelled by shortages to devise ways of getting by without depending on outside resources. At the Yanan museum one can see an abacus made from peach pits and a shallow pan of sand used for practicing writing with just one's finger.

Today this spirit of self-reliance continues. In rural areas the slogan "learn from Dazhai" does not refer simply to employing certain techniques, but to using what is at hand to increase production. Various industrial processes are being set up in the rural communes so that peasants can learn the basics of mechanization.

Some help from the outside is needed but the system of bringing in experts to do things for the peasants is discouraged. College trained persons are often referred to as "foreign (*yang*) experts" if they go into a village with a know-it-all attitude. "Native" (*tu*) experts are trained from among the villagers themselves. Peasants can combine their accumulated wisdom with new technology.

Self-reliance is combined with antielitism. Knowledge is shared, and specialists are not put on a pedestal. In medical work, for example, the doctor does not maintain a mystical superiority. Doctors, nurses, "barefoot doctors" (paramedics), and technicians form teams, and all are called "medical workers." A doctor will handle a bedpan, and a paramedic will prescribe medicines. In a hotel, for another example, all the staff will participate in cleaning and making beds, and all will participate in discussions of management policy and service.

Community life. The collective lifestyle is not only a matter of controlling selfish individualistic tendencies, but of providing a community of shared responsibility and fun. The staff at a hotel not only share in all the work, they have also been known to joke with foreign guests and challenge them to a game of ping-pong or basketball.

Every work unit, rural or urban, will have numerous activities for groups—sports, folksinging and dancing, drama groups, classes for young and old in a variety of subjects. It is possible for factory workers to do a university engineering course. Others will be given some time off work to participate in technologically oriented courses that can help improve factory production.

There are women's groups to help educate those who were deprived of education in an earlier period. Women are encouraged to increase their level of knowledge and expertise and to overcome any hesitancy they might have about joining in political discussion sessions. Child care centers allow both husband and wife to participate fully in political and productive pursuits. The rearing of children is seen as a community responsibility as well as a family one.

The aged remain active in many ways. Uncles and aunts help with child care. Old people are invited to schools to tell students of their experiences in the bitter past and to share their native knowledge. Most old people continue to live in the community rather than go to retirement homes.

Workers are respected. The distinction between workers and students is played down. Students participate in factory work and factory workers attend classes. The practical knowledge that workers gain through experience is utilized in the educational system. High school science students, for example, will go to a pumping station for a lecture from the workers on how the irrigation system works. This practical knowledge, related to the daily food of the students, will be integrated with the scientific principles they are studying.

The whole society is a learning society. Everyone seems to be involved in study, regardless of age or background. An attempt is made to involve people in courses in literacy, science, music, art, literature, medicine, politics, and philosophy. People are refreshed and grow through a constant process of learning new things.

Class hatred. One reason why old people retell stories of the bitter past is to instill a sense of class hatred in the minds of young people. Children should "grow up happily" in the new society, it is said, but they are also heirs of the revolution and need to be taught class hatred. "Remember the bitterness of the past, then you will realize the sweetness of today," children are taught, and "Remember class hatred, then you will raise your consciousness."[9]

This use of class hatred in the teaching of children may jar Western ears, but to the Chinese it is part and parcel of the collective lifestyle. In the past, people suffered because the greed of some led to poverty and starvation for others. If such greed should take hold again, the bitter past could be repeated. Class hatred means righteous anger against the inhumanity of the old system. It also means a continued intense struggle against attitudes in self or others that would foster a return of the gross inequalities of the former order. Class hatred is a hatred of the class system.

Lei Feng, it will be remembered, was able to move beyond a sense of personal revenge toward a particular landlord who had caused death and suffering for the boy's family to class hatred and a sense of the worldwide struggle against all the forces of oppression.

"Class hatred" in Chinese carries a positive connotation of opposing personal and corporate avarice. The enjoyment of life in collective communities would be completely undermined if a vigilant opposition to avarice were not maintained. Class hatred is therefore an essential element of the Maoist lifestyle.

Basic honesty and anticonsumerism. Consumerism, the desire to attain more and more possessions and pleasures for oneself, is resisted in China. Within the community there is a relatively fair distribution of goods and relatively equal access to health care, education, and other social resources. One of the benefits of life in China is the absence of a continual bombardment of advertising urging people to buy more and more things. There are no commercials on television or radio or in the other media.

The absence of consumerism reinforces basic honesty. It reduces the temptation to get more goods that one cannot afford and the urge to cheat, lie, or steal. Crime is not absent, but the rejection of the idea that all people are out for themselves has helped to reduce the motivation for deception, fraud, and petty thievery. The Maoist lifestyle has gone a long way toward achieving a society in which sharing rather than hoarding is the norm.

Criticism and self-criticism. People in their collective units engage in criticism and self-criticism sessions in order to deal with problems of selfishness and individualism that may undermine community spirit. The example of the young automobile factory worker discussed above is a case where workers criticized wrong attitudes in order to bring the young man into unity with the group.

Work units also discuss the impact of their policies and decisions on the larger society. It might be possible for a commune to plant cash crops in order to increase commune income. It has to be questioned in such a case whether the motivation is narrow group interest or concern for the needs of the larger community. Conflicts of interest arise over and over again and are dealt with in group discussion.

The need for criticism and self-criticism does not diminish as collective life develops. Contradictions, as we have said, are a permanent feature of life in Mao's view, and they will arise in each person's thought and in every group process. In criticism sessions contradictions are brought to the surface rather than allowed to fester. The unity of the group is always fragile and can be maintained only by struggling openly to resolve the conflicts and work out the wrong attitudes that inevitably arise.

The method of criticism and self-criticism is also used in dealing with disputes between various organizations. The following mundane example shows how this process works out. It was told to a visiting group by workers at a grain store in Suzhou:

This time the grain store workers told us about a dispute they had had with a factory several blocks away. The grain store processes flour and rice into wrappers for varieties of Chinese dumplings. . . . One afternoon the month before, someone called from the factory cafeteria to order a large number of one kind of dumpling wrapper to be ready by three p.m. They were made, but by five that afternoon no one had come to collect them. Meanwhile the regular supplies of dumpling wrappers had been sold out and customers were asking for them. It was too late to make any more that day, so the grain store workers sold the wrappers; and of course the factory workers appeared soon after.

"There were some hard feelings," one man from the grain store told us. "But we talked it over and decided that it was our fault—the factory workers had been involved in a long meeting and they couldn't get away to call us. If we had called them we would have found out the reason and kept the wrappers or maybe even taken them over to the factory. In any case, some of us volunteered to go over and talk to the people at the factory, and the factory thought this was a generous attitude to take, so they began to offer criticisms of themselves. By the time we finished talking, everything was all right again—and we really learned something. After that we would call before we sold an order."

This "happy ending" was a practical working arrangement; and it also demonstrated one advantage of group discussions: a single person might be very unwilling to blame himself in order to solve the problems with the factory cafeteria; but when the whole grain store discussed the issue and took responsibility as a group, criticism was seen as a constructive step toward better business practices within the store and led to a new procedure for dealing with the problem, not to mention a sense of increased solidarity with the factory workers.[10]

The interesting thing about this example is that it shows how the self-criticism process is helpful in normal, everyday disputes, and not just in earth-shaking political conflicts.

Mao study. In criticism sessions and in other group discussions people often turn to Mao's writings for guidance and inspiration. Individual and group study of Mao's thought is a characteristic of the lifestyle of people in China today. In this study there is an attempt to grapple with the meaning of life and history, to judge one's own actions and thoughts in the light of life's meaning, and to rededicate oneself to the common quest for a better world.

Many of Mao's works deal with such things as military strategy, philosophical topics like dialectical materialism, or with national and international policy. Other speeches and essays, however, raise questions very close to the daily life of the people. These writings sum up the wisdom and experience of the people involved in revolutionizing and renewing their society.

"The Foolish Old Man Who Removed Mountains," for example, is a fable Mao used to suggest the need for hard work to remove the "mountains" of imperialism and feudalism. In one rural production brigade this essay was studied during a discussion about changing the course of a river in order to reclaim a large section of fertile land. Through study of this essay the peasants were able to overcome their timidity in depending only on their own ingenuity and strength to deal with a massive problem. They devised a way of pumping water to a small reservoir above the new channel they were cutting; they loosened the soil with dynamite and then allowed the water to rush down carrying the soil into the river. It took over a year of hard work, but they were able finally to accomplish the task, encouraged by their study of Mao. One old farmer working on the project summed up what this essay of Mao meant to him:

It is necessary to struggle against nature, to struggle against class enemies, and to struggle against selfishness in our minds. We cannot assume an easygoing and comfortable lifestyle. The road to socialist construction is no peaceful journey, but one full of hard struggle.[11]

Another work of Mao's studied in this way is "Serve the People," a memorial address given for a worker who died on the job in Yanan. Today, serving the people is seen as a way to individual fulfillment. The story is told in one village of how this speech of Mao's changed the life of a crippled man:

He is a cripple, and all his life he didn't work much, for the tasks around here mean a lot of walking up and down hills and hard labor. But two years ago, during the Cultural Revolution study classes, he decided he wanted to do something. So he gathered waste wood and bits of metal, and fashioned them into turnip graters. In northwest China, we all eat turnips—so in one year he made three thousand of these to sell for the collective. Before everyone had pitied him and called him useless, but now they say, "A useless person took useless material and turned it into wealth." Now he feels so much better.[12]

The turnip graters were not for personal profit. The cripple had had his needs met by the collective. Out of a desire to serve the people he made a contribution to the village and also gained a new sense of personal worth. This is what Mao study means in the life of ordinary people in China.

Ritual and remembrance. Ritual is part of the lifestyle in China today. Great rallies are held not only in the Tiananmen square in Peking, but in most major cities on festive occasions such as National Day (October 1) and Labor Day (May 1). The study of Mao's writings also has a ritualistic flavor at times. The purpose of ritual is to give expression to group solidarity and to arouse enthusiasm for common tasks.

A family might gather around a portrait of Chairman Mao, read some quotations and sing a revolutionary song before starting the day's work. In the evening they may again gather and discuss the day's activities in light of Mao's teachings about service and struggle. In such family meetings current events and news documents are sometimes studied. Family problems are also discussed.[13]

Group reading of Mao's works helps give people a sense of unity with the nation. Peasants working to open up lonely waste areas put up a portrait of Mao to remind themselves that they are not alone. Their work has significance as part of the whole national effort.

Part of the purpose of ritual is also to recall the past and to affirm the revolutionary effort to move beyond those bitter days. The "meal of bitter remembering" is an almost sacramental ritual. One description of this kind of meal is in the story of Aunt Liang, a peasant woman who invited a group of urban students who had joined the commune to her house for such a "celebration." One of the students described the occasion:

On the other side [of the room] a space was reserved for recalling the bitter past. . . . There were some pictures and exhibits which compared their miserable life in the old society with the happy life in the new. Among these exhibits a carrying-pole especially struck the eyes of the guests, a pole which for three long generations had been saturated with sweat and rubbed smooth by many shoulders. All these made an impression on the students.

The dinner was served—wild vegetable soup, steamed bran and husks! The students understood what this dinner meant at once. Aunt Liang looked around and said with deep emotion: "Children, take and eat. . . . " No sooner had she spoken than tears raced into her eyes and streamed down her cheeks. With so many bitter grievances recalled to her mind, she began to tell of her sufferings in the old society. . . .

The new commune members had had a vivid lesson in class education. They were deeply moved as they ate the soup and bran and husks. No, what they ate was not simply a kind of food. It symbolized the blood and tears of the laboring people and their deep hatred for the old society.[14]

This meal is always celebrated by eating some of the coarse food or husks that the peasants in the past often had to eat just to survive. Sometimes it is followed by a full meal of the good food that is available to them today. It is a dramatic recollection of life in the old society. Through this ritual people are reminded that the development of a new lifestyle of sharing, struggle, and service needs to go on in order to prevent the old system of exploitation from emerging again.

In summary, the descriptions and stories in this section give us a glimpse of lifestyle in China today. A community spirit has been created in which people are encouraged to participate in the building of a world in which personal fulfillment is found through working together for the common good. Life is simple and the work is hard. Problems and disputes arise requiring criticism and self-criticism in the search for a higher unity. There is hatred of the class system and a constant recalling of harsh realities of former exploitation. This serves to increase the dedication of people to the creation of a better way of life. Individualism and selfishness are seen as the root causes of the old suffering and every effort is made to prevent such attitudes from taking control again.

The examples given are all fairly positive. No doubt the Mao study sometimes becomes formalistic, and resistance to hard work and criticism and collective goals no doubt occurs. Some people still want to leave and even risk their lives swimming to Hong Kong. Campaigns to encourage selflessness are still necessary. The examples given and many other accounts and observations indicate, however, that this new lifestyle has taken root in Chinese society and that the spirit of plain living and hard struggle has won wide acceptance throughout the nation. Many people seem to have found personal satisfaction in the noncompetitive, nonconsumerist system which China is developing.

The maintaining of a selfless lifestyle is probably most difficult for those who are in special positions of leadership, or for artists, writers, and educators who are not involved in basic production. Before evaluating the Maoist lifestyle further we will look at the special problems of such persons.

The Cadre Problem

A society needs leaders, administrators, scientists, artists, writers, educators, and doctors. In general, these occupations require special training over a period of years. How are "professional" people, and those studying professional courses, to participate in the new lifestyle? Traditionally those who work with their minds rather than with their hands achieve special privileges. Is it possible to break down the distinction between mental and manual labor? Can a system be devised in which students study in order to gain new skills with which to serve better, rather than to gain prestige, personal comforts, and better incomes? This is the cadre (*ganbu*) problem.

In its primary sense "cadre" refers to anyone in an administrative position, or anyone who works for a government or party organization.[15] By extension it is also used for all those—teachers, writers, and so forth—who are not directly engaged in physical labor.

As the term developed in revolutionary areas, where those in leadership positions were also at the forefront of the struggle, cadre came to have the connotation of more than average commitment. In time, confusion crept in. Ideally all leaders should be firm revolutionaries, but after liberation many administrators and educators were incorporated into the new system who had no particular revolutionary background. There was also a tendency to consider university graduates to be cadres simply because of their training.[16] At the same time it was still said that cadres were those "who devote themselves heart and soul to the service of the people."[17]

This confusion is at the very heart of the cadre problem. China trains people to fill certain intellectually oriented tasks. These people become leaders. Professional qualifications alone, however, do not make a cadre. The problem is how to develop people who are both academically qualified to do their jobs and also dedicated to unselfish service. Cadres should not form a special class. Workers and peasants should have access to education on an equal basis with those who come from cadre backgrounds. It is necessary both to train cadres so that they will put service above self, and for cadres to develop a continuing lifestyle of frugality close to the people.

Red and expert. As we have said, the term "red" refers to commitment to the goals of the revolution—building a society without exploitation and special privileges for any class or group. To be red is to be unselfish, to be ethically sensitive, to act and live in a style consistent with socialist egalitarianism. The person who has expertise but lacks redness will tend to use his or her skill for personal, private goals.[18]

The term "red" may be meaningless to most Westerners. Perhaps it would be more relevant if we substituted "filled with human concern and dedication." If we were choosing a medical doctor, for example, we would want a person who is skilled and who also has a sincere concern for people.

The "red and expert" problem is not as foreign to our own situations as might appear at first glance. We may have resigned ourselves to the fact that those who heal and teach and administer our government and industry seek and receive money, status, and other benefits far above that of the world's poor. We may even accept this as the natural order of society. If we look at ourselves, we will probably find that we accept this competitive system and are motivated by the desire to live a little better, get our children into better schools, and have the homes, vacations, cars, and appliances that the system teaches us to desire.

The Maoists reject this approach. The persons who have access to the education that will give them special skills should be red and expert. They should not allow themselves to look upon officials and educators and managers as superior to those who plow, or labor on the docks, or work on assembly lines, or collect garbage, or wait on tables.

The well-tempered cadre. Over a long period of years there has developed an ideal of what a cadre should be—an ideal which not all cadres live up to, obviously. Cadres should be tempered through struggle for the revolution. They should be heroes or heroines of daring and selflessness, able to resist the degenerate philosophy of personal success. They should set a moral example. Early in the revolution Mao commented on how the leaders of the peasant movement, these potential cadres, forced the gentry to give up opium and how they stood against gambling, frivolity, vulgarity, and waste.[19]

The cadre should not be characterized by petty-bourgeois selfishness, Mao later wrote, but by "largeness of mind." He should be "staunch and active, looking upon the interests of the revolution as his very life and subordinating his personal interests to those of the revolution."[20] Party cadres should play an exemplary role:

They should be true in word and resolute in deed, free from arrogance and sincere. . . . Every Communist engaged in government work should set an example of absolute integrity, of freedom from favoritism in making appointments and of hard work for little remuneration. Every Communist working among the masses should be their friend and not a boss over them, an indefatigable teacher and not a bureaucratic politician. At no time and in no circumstances should a Communist place his personal interests first; he should subordinate them to the interests of the nation and of the masses. Hence selfishness, slacking, corruption, seeking the limelight, and so on, are most contemptible, while selflessness, working with all one's energy, whole-hearted devotion to public duty, and quiet hard work will command respect. . . . It must be realized that Communists form only a small section of the nation. . . . It is entirely wrong to think that we alone are good and no one else is any good. . . . In a long war and in adverse circumstances, the dynamic energy of the whole nation can be mobilized in the struggle to overcome difficulties, defeat the enemy and build a new China only if the Communists play an exemplary role to the best of their abilities together with all the advanced elements among the friendly parties and armies and among the masses.[21]

After the victory of the revolutionary war the effort continued to promote correct attitudes among those in leadership positions. A rural commune leader was written about as an example of one who maintains a simple life close to the people. He regularly participates in collective work in order "to keep his thinking pure." Through the heat of the summer and the cold of the winter he works side by side with the commune members. At the office each day he sweeps the floor and the adjoining street and courtyard. Afterwards he carries a manure basket on his head as he proceeds to the fields to work. He visits the peasants regardless of rain or snow and helps them with problems that arise. He maintains "a style of plain living and hard work." His clothes are old and patched but his mind is "clearly guided by Mao Tse-tung Thought."[22]

Ideal cadres, then, are not arrogant, do not hesitate to get involved in physical labor and dirty work, maintain good and close relations with those in their unit, do not expect to be waited on and have special privileges, and do their jobs well. The fact that some cadres are lifted up as good examples indicates that not all cadres are like this. Statistical evidence is not available, but by simple reasoning it can be said that the features of a cadre lifestyle that are highlighted for teaching purposes are the features where distortions and corruption appear.

Cadre distortions of the struggle ethic. Cadres have connections with other people in authority. They may use their positions and contacts to get better housing, special school places for their children, and other privileges.

Some young people have the attitude that one should study in order to become a cadre and get ahead in life. They do not want to do farm work, even if that is what the society needs. "Their sole desire is to study in the higher middle schools and universities and become cadres." This attitude was especially prevalent in the early years after liberation. Some girl students, in order to avoid agricultural labor, went to the cities "to make indiscreet love to men." Other students contemplated suicide if they could not escape farm work by passing the higher middle school entrance examination.[23] Such young people saw advanced education only in terms of the personal gain they would get from it.

Sometimes the distortion is more subtle. Students may go to the countryside not out of dedication, but as a step toward getting ahead. Liu Shaoqi was criticized during the Cultural Revolution for having encouraged such impure motives. Some students had told Liu that they did not want to go to the rural areas because it would be detrimental to their careers. Liu then suggested to them that they work on farms for three to five years and learn all the peasants knew about farming. Combining this knowledge with their school education and with the respect they would earn for having "sacrificed" themselves to become farmers, they would be in an advantageous position to become local officials. This would put them on the ladder leading up to provincial and national positions. Liu's approach was criticized as insincere, "giving up a little in order to gain much."[24]

Older cadres also try such tricks or engage in tokenism. All people engaged in mental work—writers, artists, doctors, administrators—are under strong social pressure to spend periods of time in physical labor, especially in the countryside where work is the most difficult. Sometimes such work becomes mere tokenism; thus it is called gold-plating. Tempering quality steel is a long process, but gold-plating takes only a dip.[25] Some people in cadre positions go to the countryside to do a bit of farm work for "show." One medical doctor went to a commune for a short period with the hope of achieving "prestige as a revolutionary." His wrong motivations were exposed when he recoiled from shoveling manure and doing hard work. A similar thing developed with an art performer who did rural work only "to get the veneer of progressiveness."[26]

The Maoist system does not suggest that society can get along without leaders, specialists, and experts. The cadre problem cannot be solved by eliminating cadres. It is felt, however, that cadres do not inevitably have to become a new class, like the officials, intellectuals, specialists, and bureaucrats in the old society. What is needed is an attitude and a lifestyle for cadres that will help them remain close to the common people.

Correcting cadre distortions. A number of methods have been developed in China that attempt to correct cadre arrogance, selfishness, gold-plating, and bureaucratism. One of these is the method of self-criticism. The leader of a unit participates with others in criticism and self-criticism sessions, which provide the opportunity for checking individual behavior in light of common goals. Resentments and problems that have been festering can be brought to the surface and worked out.

The method of self-criticism has been worked out over a long period of years as an integral part of revolutionary lifestyle. We discussed above the use of self-criticism among workers and peasants in various units. It is especially important in the life of cadres. Mao has written about the importance of self-criticism within the Party, but the same ideas apply to other cadres as well:

Conscientious practice of self-criticism is still another hallmark distinguishing our Party from all other political parties. As we say, dust will accumulate if a room is not cleaned regularly, our faces will get dirty if they are not washed. Our comrades' minds and our Party's work may also collect dust, and also need sweeping and washing. . . . To check up regularly on our work and in the process develop a democratic style of work, to fear neither criticism nor self-criticism . . . is the only efficient way to prevent all kinds of political dust and germs from contaminating the minds of our comrades. . . . As we Chinese Communists, who base all our actions on the highest interests of the broadest masses of the Chinese people and who are fully convinced of the justice of our cause, never balk at any personal sacrifice and are ready at all times to give our lives for the cause, can we be reluctant to discard any idea, viewpoint, opinion or method which is not suited to the needs of the people.[27]

The method of self-criticism is not easy. It requires basic unity, mutual trust, and openness within the group. These, however, do not always prevail. Some persons will be intent on exposing others' faults, but unwilling to criticize their own. Competitiveness, an immature inability to accept any leadership, and the attitude that "only I am correct," have a negative impact on the criticism process. Some people seize the mistakes of others, which are exposed in self-criticism, and use them for making petty attacks. Insecure cadres hesitate to do self-criticism out of fear of appearing weak or of losing face.

To counteract such fears, self-criticism is heralded by the Maoists as a "glorious tradition" and a "noble revolutionary style of work." It is said that since it requires courage to expose one's errors in public a person will gain in stature rather than lose face through the process. Doing self-criticism will help to overcome bad work styles and will lead to closer ties between the leaders and the led. To be afraid to do self-criticism is seen as selfish, putting one's own interests above those of the community. "Anyone who is afraid to engage in self-criticism is afraid to wage self-revolution and afraid to touch himself to the depths of his soul. This is a result of putting 'self' above everything else."

In order to develop an atmosphere of trust, a criticism session should not be an accusation session. It should begin with persons criticizing their own faults and mistakes first. Then they might discuss others' faults in a spirit of unity.[28]

Public self-criticism could lead to undue conformity. It is not the ethical ideal, but no doubt some people conform in the self-criticism process simply to avoid trouble for themselves.[29] Ideally one should be independent in one's thought (*duli sikao*) and oppose the group if it is believed that in so doing one will advance the revolution. It is obviously difficult to know when one is acting selfishly in opposing the group or acting selfishly in going along with it. For one to oppose Party authorities whom one thinks have taken the capitalist road is an act of courage and selflessness. Many people have been commended for taking this step.

Self-criticism is an imperfect tool which can itself be misused. Nevertheless it plays an important role in the development of a cadre lifestyle that is free from arrogance, insensitivity to the people's needs, and self-seeking.

Another method of correcting cadre distortions of the struggle ethic is to have them spend time in manual labor close to the workers and peasants. Students, who may become cadres, also spend time in ordinary physical labor.

Since the Cultural Revolution university students are recruited from among the workers and peasants. All high school graduates go to work in factories or on farms. Those who wish to apply for advanced study have to be recommended by their fellow workers. They are also screened by representatives from the university, although no formal examination is given. It is planned that in this way all workers and peasants will have relatively equal access to higher education. Children from cadre families will also have two or more years experience as farmers or factory workers before proceeding with their education. This represents another attempt to break down the barriers between potential cadres and ordinary workers.

Going to work on farms can be a difficult and purifying experience for someone from an urban area who has never been in contact with peasant life. It can help in overcoming attitudes of superiority and give a more realistic understanding of the daily lives of the 80 percent of China's people who are farmers. The transformation of one urban youth is captured in his account of such an experience:

Once, when I helped poor peasant Liu Cheng-yi clean a pigsty, I hesitated because of the dirt. But Liu Cheng-yi rolled up his trouserlegs, took off his shoes and jumped into the pigsty to begin the work. He said to me: "I will work inside the sty and you work outside so that you will not get your clothes dirty." I thought of Chairman Mao's teaching while I worked: "In the last analysis, the workers and peasants were the cleanest people and even though their hands were soiled and their feet smeared with cow-dung, they were really cleaner than the bourgeois and petty-bourgeois intellectuals."

Examining myself in the light of Chairman Mao's teaching, I became aware of my wrong thinking. Liu Cheng-yi worked inside the pigsty and I worked outside; this meant that there was a wall between us. And this was not an ordinary wall either, but one which prevented me from integrating with the poor peasants. I must pull it down once and for all! I plucked up my courage and jumped into the pigsty. Smiling to himself, Liu Cheng-yi said, "Now you are like a child of the poor peasants!"[30]

One jump into a pigsty does not mean total transformation of world outlook, but the accumulation of such experiences by thousands of cadres and students is bound to go a long way toward overcoming cadre distortions.

Cadres have always been encouraged to engage in manual labor, but this took on a definitive form in the Cultural Revolution. Special Cadre Schools[31] were set up and it was expected that all who were in the cadre category would spend six months or more in such schools.

These Cadre Schools have been organized by various branches of the government at national, provincial, and municipal levels. They are in rural areas, usually using a tract of marginal land not already under cultivation. The task of the first generation of cadre-students is to build dormitories and other necessary buildings, to begin the hard work of making the land productive, and to set up handicraft shops. These shops use only scrap materials. The idea is that the Cadre School will be self-supporting and will not be a drain on national resources.

The purpose of the Cadre School is not to punish, but to give time for work and reflection. Part of the day is spent in manual labor and part in study and discussion. The labor helps the cadres to remember that mental work does not make them superior to physical laborers. The study gives time to reflect on what the lifestyle of a cadre should be. After a period of time in the school it is expected that the cadres will return to their work with a more sensitive understanding of the common people and with greater dedication to building a society in which the leaders and administrators are not a privileged class.

One cadre told the story of how he had become accustomed to a soft life in his government department. He had a car to take him to meetings, someone brought him tea at his desk, and he had other privileges that made him think of himself as superior to ordinary workers. One of his first tasks at the Cadre School was to go back to the urban district where he had worked to collect night soil from the houses to use as fertilizer. He had to push a manure cart and call for the people to bring the night soil buckets to the door. From shame and embarrassment he almost lost his voice and found it difficult to call out. Over a period of time, he came to realize that this was because of his own attitude of superiority. Eventually he was able to deal with the problem. He recalled that he had carried manure and worked in the fields during the revolutionary civil war and had never thought it to be an inferior task. Years of work as a government official had caused him to become arrogant. Through the experience in the Cadre School he was eventually able to go back to his job a better cadre.[32]

Participation in physical labor plays an important role in the transformation of thought and character. In one Cadre School students said they preferred to use hoes to turn the earth rather than use tractors in plowing. "Machines can work for us," they are reported to have said, "but they cannot transform our thought."[33] When they are back on their regular jobs the cadres continue to participate in physical labor. Depending on the demands of their jobs this might be for a part of each day, or one day a week, or a month every half year. Leaders of the Party, Army, and government do part-time labor with workers and peasants in order to "knit the leaders closely together with the masses," and to keep those in positions of authority from bureaucratism and from taking on the "airs of a lord."[34]

This kind of physical labor is also open to distortions similar to the "gold-plating" described above. If, however, it is done consistently, over a long period of time, with periods of time in a Cadre School where physical work, study, and reflection are combined, then there is some hope of avoiding tokenism.

A system in which leaders, professional people, and educators go to factories and farms and Cadre Schools to work and reflect is so foreign to our Western societies that it is difficult to evaluate the emotions involved. One has difficulty

conjuring up a picture of senators, mayors, university professors, corporation executives, admirals, movie stars, writers,
and lawyers in our own society spending 20 percent of their
time picking grapes, assembling tractors, carrying manure,
baling hay, and learning from workers and farmers. The social
systems are entirely different, and such labor may not by itself
lead to a decisive transformation. But even granting a great
mixture of motivations on the part of our "cadres," we could
expect at least some instances of very basic attitudinal change
through such labor.

The study of Mao's thought is also seen as a method of
correcting cadre distortions of the struggle ethic. This does not
mean only studying Mao's theories about contradiction and
revolution as a philosophical discipline, but of using Mao's
teachings as a standard for judging one's actions. Mao study is
normally a group process in which various teachings are used
in the discussion of everyday problems and the world situation.
In some ways it is comparable to religious study of the Scrip-
tures as a way of lifting one's horizons and developing one's
character and sense of dedication.

Mao asks the ethical question of whom one serves. Cadres
are reminded that their work should serve the common people. Mao teaches unselfishness and the need to join in the hard
and dirty work of peasants. Humility and overcoming arrogance are also emphasized.

The common study of Mao's thought is said to be helpful in
achieving unity. A cadre should not just give commands, but
listen to others in a spirit of unity. Mao's thought is used as a
standard for judging both others' thinking and one's own.[35]

Mao's thought is also used to encourage people in their
continued transformation. The ethic of Mao is demanding in
what it expects of people: the overcoming of many ingrained
habits of cadre superiority. It is also hopeful, however, because
it assumes that anyone who is willing to try can make progress.

One sixty-year-old schoolteacher became very discouraged
because of criticisms from her students. She became depressed
and walked around looking glum. She felt she was too old to
change and considered giving up schoolteaching. The Party

secretary noted her condition and had "heart to heart" talks with her. Together they read Mao's teaching in which the hope was expressed that all intellectuals would be transformed and advance. The teacher was encouraged to become a friend of the workers and peasants, which she did. Under patient guidance by the Party secretary she began a spiritual change. She found new energy to struggle against her discouragement. Her attitudes changed and in time she was even honored as an outstanding teacher. She had taught for over thirty years, she said, but only now was she discovering what it is one lives for.[36]

Mao study, then, plays an important role in the daily life of cadres. It helps in the struggle against pride, self-centeredness, and wrong thoughts. It is influential in the developing of compassionate and considerate interpersonal relationships, in the midst of the common quest for meaningful life and service. Meaning is found in living for others rather than for oneself.

In summary, the cadre problem is a basic issue of how leadership and specialization is related to egalitarian goals. In actual practice cadre privileges still exist, making necessary campaigns to instill the struggle ethic in the minds of those in leadership positions or specialized fields. The transgressions against the struggle ethic, such as scheming to get better housing or schooling, may seem relatively minor compared with the privileges of persons in equivalent positions in Western societies. If not kept under control, however, the disparities would tend to become greater and greater.

Participation in self-criticism, physical labor, and Mao study, and spending periods of time in Cadre Schools, all help in the correction of distortions of the struggle ethic. No system is foolproof, however, and the issue of cadre privilege continues to arise.

The cadre problem may seem quite distant from our experience in the West, but that may only be because we have not faced the issue head on. Crime, minority resentments, women's liberation efforts, labor unrest, all reflect the struggle over who has access to jobs, resources, prestige, necessities, luxuries, and power. The Maoists, however imperfectly, are trying to deal with this issue, and cadre privilege is the nub of the matter in a socialist society. The Maoists insist that cadres will not become a new class.

Evaluation of the Maoist Lifestyle

Various people will evaluate the Maoist lifestyle differently, but a few general points can be made. There are elements of the lifestyle in China that will strike some people as strange or unattractive. Other elements may look good in theory, but seem too demanding in practice.

There is an emphasis on class hatred and militancy that at first may seem unnecessarily harsh. The Chinese lived through a century of war, deprivation, and revolution. They have identified the evils of that era with the class system and the gross inequality they witnessed. The militant rejection of that system will seem harsh to those of us who have been living in relative comfort, who have not experienced a situation that allowed famine for some while others lived in luxury. As we become sensitive to the brutalities of the present world economic structures we may be less repelled by the language of class hatred. Or at least we may be able to understand why there is such a severe rejection of the old inequalities.

Enjoying a life of relative comfort may make it difficult to appreciate the call to plain living and hard struggle. China is a poor country, although it has been able to achieve a fair enough distribution of national resources to make grinding poverty and starvation a thing of the past. If frugality were not emphasized there would be the danger of a small percentage of the population again monopolizing the limited resources.

Plain living and hard struggle may sound too ascetic to be very appealing. This emphasis in the Maoist lifestyle has sometimes been seen in China itself as frugality for the sake of frugality. Maoist writers deny this. "We are not stoics,"[37] they have written, and "we are neither ascetics nor puritans."[38] The very need for such denials is an indication of the problem. There is a rejection of luxurious living, and physical labor is seen as good for keeping one's thought pure. There is an ascetic tendency here.

The question of asceticism, however, goes back to the question of distribution. It is not that the pleasures of life are evil, but that unequal access to these pleasures is not tolerated. There is a great effort to prevent class distinctions from emerging again.

It might be said by Western observers that the Chinese are simply making a virtue out of a necessity and that when they achieve our level of affluence they will not need to emphasize plain living and hard struggle. This is only partly true. As productivity in China has increased, the goods available to all the people have also increased. It is possible to project a future of a much more abundant life for people in China. The error of this assessment is that it overlooks the unequal distribution in Western societies. To assume that the luxuries enjoyed are based simply on greater productivity is to ignore the fact that the high standard of living in the West is based both on gross inequalities in the social system and on the extraction of wealth from other parts of the world. One also must not overlook the fact that such unlimited consumption of the world's resources is an artificial lifestyle which would be impossible for all the people of the world to enjoy, and which will eventually exhaust irreplaceable resources.

Plain living and hard struggle, then, is both a realistic response to China's present level of production and a lifestyle based on an understanding that high living is always at the expense of others. There is a short-range frugality that will be eased as production increases and all the people have a greater share of life's necessities and pleasures. There is also a long-range frugality which seeks to find a way of life in balance with the resources available.

The emphasis on a simple lifestyle and hard work is related in the Chinese experience to the problem of individualism and consumerism. Happiness is not to be found, according to Mao's struggle ethic, in the amassing of more goods for oneself, but in working for the good of the total community. One Marxist writer was criticized for his view of happiness in which he said that a person "should be well-fed and clothed, should live in a spacious and clean house, and should enjoy love and life in amity with spouse, parents and children." There is nothing wrong with food, house, clothes, and family love, but it was considered too individualistic to talk only of building one's "comfortable nest" and neglecting society. In contrast to this, the Communist ideal is

. . . to eliminate classes, exploitation, the difference between mental and manual labor, the difference between workers and peasants and the difference between town and country; to raise social productivity and the ideological and cultural level of the people to a great extent, turn labor into the first need of human life, enable every person to give full play to his ability on the premise of serving the people, and enjoy a good material and spiritual life in the collective.[39]

The overcoming of individualism and selfishness is furthered by using the method of criticism and self-criticism and by emphasizing that advanced education is for the purpose of greater service and not personal gain. An individual should not have a free choice of career without reference to community needs and goals. A person should not be encouraged to get ahead, since this implies stepping on other people who are falling behind. A spirit of community cooperation rather than individual competitiveness is being nurtured.

This approach is in conflict with the social values of success, fame, wealth, and position. It may seem to some that the Maoist lifestyle is a violation of individual freedom and human rights. It may also go against a widely-understood view of human nature. What of those who cherish a right to liberty, free choice of career and place of work, and individual pursuit of happiness?

The Maoists are not opposed to liberty, happiness, and personal fulfillment, but feel that these should be found in collective rather than individualistic effort. They also feel that these liberties and opportunities are not equally accessible to everyone in Western societies, but that economic conditions determine one's life chances. This conflict of values and difference of perspective will be covered more fully in the following chapter. The Maoist approach is motivated by a desire to achieve a society where equality and community spirit are truly present. Insofar as this is the case, the conflict in values deserves careful consideration.

We may have things to learn from the Maoist lifestyle. A system of individual freedom may cause problems of poverty and injustice of which we are not conscious and which, on reflection, we may want to avoid. The moral revitalization, the selflessness of the Maoist ideal, the willingness to put community interests above personal goals, may be characteristics that would be helpful in overcoming some of the problems that many face today.

This is not to say that the Maoist lifestyle could ever be taken over totally in other societies. The West may need more social unity than it has, but there may be more unity in China than the West needs or desires. In the United States people enjoy political satire, foreign policy debates in the press, and the rough and tumble of electoral politics. Learning from the Maoist lifestyle would not necessarily threaten these.

In American traditions there has not been the same disdain for physical labor, the same deprivation of power among the common people, the same willingness to allow some in the society to starve, the same degree of class bifurcation as the Chinese experienced in their past, although Americans do suffer from injustices in many of these areas. We can learn from the Maoist experience, but the kind of transformation our own society requires is not the same as China's, and the lifestyle that will emerge from our continued struggles will reflect our own cultural heritage.

NOTES

1. SW III, p. 96.

2. SW III, p. 178.

3. SW IV, p. 374.

4. SW IV, p. 155.

5. Hsiao Hua, "Learn from the 'Good Eighth Company of Nanking Road' and Promote the Revolutionary Traditions of Plain Living and Hard Struggle," CY, no. 10–11 (May 18, 1963), SCMM, no. 372 (July 8, 1963), pp. 23–26.

6. Yuan Hsien-la, "God's Precepts and the 'Morality' of Shooting One's Neighbor," RF, nos. 21 and 22 (November 10, 1961), SCMM, no. 290 (December 4, 1961), pp. 42–43.

7. Liu Ya-sung, "Feng Ting's Books Harmed Me, Chairman Mao's Books Saved Me," *Kung-jen Jih-pao (Workers Daily)* (Peking), February 13, 1965, SCMP, no. 3422 (March 23, 1965), pp. 10–12.

8. William Hinton, "Chou En-lai" (report of an interview), *New China* 1, no. 2 (Summer 1975): 28–29.

9. Editorial, "Class Education for Children to be Given according to Their Special Characteristics," *Chung-kuo Fu-nu (Women of China)*, no. 6 (June 1, 1963), SCMM, no. 377 (August 12, 1963), p. 35.

10. Committee of Concerned Asian Scholars, *China! Inside the People's Republic* (New York: Bantam Books, 1972), pp. 54–55.

11. Ibid., pp. 40–41.

12. Ibid., p. 43.

13. "Peasant Families in North China Run Classes for the Study of Mao Tse-tung Thought," Hsinhua News Agency (Shihchiachuang), March 18, 1968, SCMP, no. 4143 (March 21, 1968), pp. 23–24.

14. Yu Jen, "Aunt Liang's Dinner Party," *Chinese Literature*, no. 12 (1968), pp. 86–87.

15. Quoted in Franz Schurmann, *Ideology and Organization in Communist China* (Berkeley: University of California Press, 1966), p. 165.

16. One article stated that Peking University, in its first decade after liberation, had "supplied the State with 7272 cadres," obviously equating university graduation with cadre status. Lu P'ing, "Peking University's Colossal Achievement During the Past Decade," *Pei-ching Ta-hsueh Hsueh-pao (Peking University Journal)*, no. 4 (1959), ECMM, no. 207 (April 11, 1960), p. 30.

17. An Tsu-wen, "A Correct Approach to the Problem of Retirement of Women Cadres," *Chung-kuo Fu-nu (Women of China)*, no. 2 (February 1, 1958), ECMM, no. 125 (April 14, 1958), p. 15.

18. Anonymous, "Peking Young Communist League Committee and Young Communist League Committee of Tsinghua University Call Separate Forums on Redness and Expertness," *CYN*, December 8, 1962, SCMP, no. 2889 (January 2, 1963), p. 3.

19. SW I, pp. 31 and 49.

20. SW II, pp. 32–33.

21. SW II, p. 198.

22. "Good Example of Cadre Who Goes to Work at Grass Roots," Hsinhua

News Agency, Chengchow, January 7, 1969, SCMP, no. 4336 (January 13, 1969), pp. 18–19.

23. Chou Li-po, "Why Does Wang Ping-yuan Get Fed Up with Rural Work and How Does Han Wen-kung Succeed in Rural Work," CY, no. 20 (1955), ECMM, no. 17 (December 5, 1955), p. 37.

24. Hsuch'ang District Correspondence Group (authors), "A Corrosive Harmful to the Soul of Youth," *Nung-ts'un Ch'ing-nien (Rural Youth),* no. 13 (July 10, 1967), SCMM, no. 599 (October 30, 1967), pp. 28–30.

25. Chien Hung, "Gold-plating and Tempering," CY, no. 2 (January 16, 1963), SCMM, no. 354 (March 4, 1963), p. 31.

26. "Remove the Backward Label through Action," and "Gold-plating: Self-Deception and an Attempt to Deceive Others," *Yang-ch'eng Wan-pao* (Canton), January 3, 1966, SCMP, no. 3618 (January 17, 1966), pp. 10–12.

27. SW III, pp. 316–17.

28. Over the decades there have been numerous articles on self-criticism. The discussion here draws on two particular articles: Editorial, "Study Conscientiously, Reform Ideology and Improve Work," *Literary Gazette* (Peking), December 10, 1951, CB, no. 156 (February 5, 1952), p. 44; and Jen Li-shin, "Everyone Should Conduct More Self-Criticism," PD, February 13, 1968, SCMP, no. 4124 (February 23, 1968), pp. 10–13.

29. For example, the editors of *China Youth* rejected an article critical of the writer Feng Ting. Later the same article appeared in the leading Party journal *Red Flag.* The editors of *China Youth* published a self-criticism that seemed to be more getting in line with a policy change they had missed than a genuine, independently arrived at critique. See editorial, "Powerful Persuasion and Encouragement: How Comrade Chang Ch'i-hsun's Criticism of Comrade Feng Ting's *Communist View of Life* Has Enlightened Us," CY, no. 20 (October 16, 1964), SCMM, no. 446 (December 7, 1963), pp. 1–5; and Editor's Notes, CB, no. 750 (January 13, 1965).

30. *Peking Review,* May 7, 1971, pp. 19–21.

31. These are called May Seventh Cadre Schools, in commemoration of a directive of Chairman Mao on May 7, 1966, urging cadres to participate in physical labor.

32. This story was told to the author on a visit to a Cadre School near Peking in 1971.

33. PD, March 20, 1970.

34. Editorial, "Why Must We 'Rectify Working Style'?" PD, May 2, 1967.

35. Sung Yang and Hsiang Yang (authors, presumably pseudonymous), "He Who Does Not Know the Meaning of Unity Does Not Know the Meaning of Revolution," KM, May 17, 1969, SCMP, no. 4432 (June 9, 1969), pp. 5–8.

36. Ibid.

37. Yang Ta-hsueh, "Be the First to Worry, the Last to Enjoy," CY, nos. 10–11 (May 18, 1963), SCMM, no. 20 (October 16, 1964), p. 8.

38. Yu T'ing, "Peddling Bourgeois Contraband under the Signboard of Communism: A Review of Comrade Feng Ting's Book, *Communist View of Life,*" CY, no. 20 (October 16, 1964), SCMM, no. 446 (December 7, 1964), p. 8.

39. Kan Feng, "What Philosophy of Life is This?: On Comrade Feng Ting's *Communist Philosophy of Life,*" CYN, October 31, 1964, CB, no. 750 (January 13, 1965), p. 5.

CHAPTER 5

THE STRUGGLE ETHIC
AND LIBERAL VALUES

At various points our discussion has touched on the conflict
between Maoist values and the liberal values of Western society. In this chapter we will deal more directly with the Maoist
critique of these liberal values.

There is no neat way of dealing with this problem. We do not
have an "objective" standpoint from which we can view both
Maoist and liberal values. It would be possible simply to maintain a liberal view, but the Maoists reject this world view as
representative of the exploiting classes. It would be artificial
and distorting at the other extreme to try to jump into the
Maoist mentality and look at liberal values from a Maoist
standpoint.

It is almost impossible to avoid a liberal mentality in framing
the issues. We try to look at the Maoist critique of liberal values
as an intellectual problem that can be "solved" through reading or writing books and articles. The Maoist would say that
what is at stake here is not an academic point of argument but
questions of oppression, justice, struggle, and conflict. The
issues can be resolved, from a Maoist point of view, only

113

through a revolutionary struggle against oppression and not through a scholarly debate. It is precisely academic debates, abstracted from the struggle for justice, that the Maoists criticize and condemn.

For the sake of honesty we will have to sacrifice neatness. We are Western liberals trying to understand an ethic that seems to reject our whole world view. The Maoists say that it is impossible to understand the struggle for justice from the viewpoint of liberalism, since liberalism represents the bourgeoisie, the perpetrators of injustice. We can deny this Maoist evaluation of liberalism, but to do so would simply be to make a liberal critique of Maoism.

There are two aspects of a less than neat solution to this impasse. First, we can agree to link the quest for understanding to the quest for justice. We can try to put ourselves at least among the wavering, dissatisfied, petty-bourgeois intellectuals who support the struggle for justice. Perhaps we have been subjected to economic, racist, or sexist injustices, or at least have shared the sufferings of others who have been. A glimmer may get through to us of what class struggle and revolution mean to those who suffer. Without playing fanciful games we can perhaps say that, however inadequately lived, we stand with the oppressed, therefore we understand.

Second, we can also make an effort, without any pretensions about being Maoist revolutionaries and without denying our bourgeois liberal mentality, to enter as far as possible into a Maoist world view. We can try to see the world from the point of view of the struggle ethic, recognizing that our vision will be partial and limited. Making the effort may lead to an increased understanding of the thrust of the Maoist rejection of liberal values.

What are the liberal values? They are so much a part of the air we breathe that we tend to take them for granted. Among the values to be discussed below are liberalism, the theory of human nature, freedom, equality, love, and the liberal view of truth.

In Maoist writings the liberal values are rejected. From the point of view of the struggle ethic these values do not realistically reflect the problem of power or the class struggle for justice in the contemporary world. The liberal values, it is said, are expressed in terms of humanity, but in practice serve the interests of one class, the bourgeoisie.

The Maoist Critique of Liberal Values

Liberalism. Liberalism means, among other things, a willingness to be objective, fair, tolerant, open-minded. It is the opposite of doctrinaire, narrow, ideological. Most Western learning is based on the idea that responsible scholarship requires a liberal attitude. One should not prejudge a situation but make a careful decision after having all the available evidence in hand.

Robert Jay Lifton, in his study of thought reform in China, criticizes the Maoist approach because it is, in Lifton's view, contrary to liberalism. Lifton sees liberalism as the desire for moderation, the willingness to live and let live, consideration for both sides of any question, "gradualism," consideration of human feelings, tolerance for human frailty, respect for individual differences, and concern for other people as individuals.[1] He finds these qualities, some of which he says are also traditional Chinese values, lacking in Chinese Communism.

What would the Maoist response to such criticism be? First, it would be asked, when did the bourgeoisie show liberal attitudes toward the poor peasants and workers? In the starvation and exploitation which were part of old China, when was the desire for moderation and concern for human frailty expressed by those in powerful positions? It would be said also that liberalism may characterize relationships among the educated elite, but these benefits are not extended to the illiterate people who do the backbreaking work of society.

The Maoists would feel no need to defend the revolution from liberal critics, since Maoists reject liberalism as a sham. In his 1937 essay "Combat Liberalism," Mao expresses the opinion that liberalism simply covers over real problems without facing them squarely. The liberal attitude, he says, is to "let things slide for the sake of peace and friendship," and to "let things drift if they do not affect one personally." In other words, a facade is maintained in order to keep relationships smooth even when there is an issue which should be dealt with.

Mao writes that the liberal approach leads people to reject discipline, to hear incorrect views expressed without rebutting them, to see persons doing things that harm the interests of the common people and yet not react, to place personal concerns first, and to be opportunistic.[2]

It is instructive to compare Mao's view of liberalism with that of Lifton's. Where Lifton praises liberalism for its gradualism and live-and-let-live attitude, Mao condemns these very same features of liberalism for letting things drift and not being indignant about activities that are harmful to the people. Lifton's "consideration for human feelings" is seen by Mao as preserving superficial peace and friendship rather than confronting conflict issues. Lifton's "tolerance for human frailty" and "respect for individual differences" become for Mao the attitude of putting personal interests above revolutionary interests.

The basic difference is really in terms of class perspective. From the point of view of those who are suffering exploitation, the niceties of gradualism, live-and-let-live, and "seeing both sides of the question" simply dodge the real issues. Liberalism can be practiced by bourgeois intellectuals because they are not the ones being stepped on in society. To the poor worker or peasant, "seeing both sides of the question" is the academic's method of not taking sides in the struggle for power and justice. This is why Mao sees the liberal attitude as opportunistic. It is an approach that tries to stand above the conflict, but such a stand is a luxury available only to those who are not oppressed. To stand above the battle is to stand with those who are benefitting unfairly from the system, the rich and powerful exploiters.

Some Western writers, sympathetic with Marxism, oppose the antiliberalism that Mao's thought represents. They claim that Marx encompassed liberal humanist values in his writings but that these have been lost or distorted by Communist regimes in both Russia and China. Erich Fromm and C. Wright Mills take this approach.

Erich Fromm attempts to explicate the real meaning of Marxism, as opposed to the "pseudo-Marxism" of Russia and China.[3] Marx was not primarily concerned with economic exploitation, says Fromm, but with the liberation of persons from alienation. Human existence is alienated from essence, persons are not what they "ought to be." The capitalist mode of production is the real enemy, according to Fromm's interpretation, because it represents the highest degree of alienation. Both the capitalist and the worker are victims of this system which they have created. In socialism, both will be liberated, self-alienation will be abolished, and persons will become fully human, free individuals.[4]

C. Wright Mills, who puts Mao among the "revisionists," considers Karl Marx to be close to the liberal humanists. Marx criticized liberal society of his day, writes Mills, using as the basis of his critique the very moral values proclaimed by that society itself—that is, liberty, equality, reason, progress.[5] Liberalism and Marxism share a common set of ideals or values, according to Mills, but liberalism simply mouths these values, lacking any viable plan for realizing them. Liberalism has become opportunistic, rhetoric for defending the status quo.[6] Mills's thesis is that classical Marxism might be able to make up for the deficiencies of liberalism.

In his exposition of Marxism, Mills uses the concept of alienation in its noneconomic sense, as does Fromm. For Mills, alienation is psychological rather than material deprivation. Alienation is not rooted in the capitalist mode of production, in Mills's view but "the facts of mass industrialization itself." It is found in both capitalist and noncapitalist societies. The enemy, in Mills's analysis, is not exploiters or imperialists, but mass technology.[7]

The writers who try to put Marx in the liberal or humanist camp avoid the central issue of revolutionary class struggle. They focus on alienation as a problem facing humankind rather than on oppression as a problem facing the poor and wretched of the earth. This interpretation of Marxism is unacceptable to the Maoists. For the Maoists there is an essential conflict between liberalism and Marxism. In the Maoist interpretation, liberalism and humanism must be opposed because they emasculate the ethic of struggle. They put the exploiter and the exploited in the same boat, over against the capitalist mode of production or mass technology.

As an example of this issue, take the question of apartheid. The liberal may say that apartheid is dehumanizing for both the whites and the blacks living under this system. It plainly would be in error, however, to say that because the system is dehumanizing for both whites and blacks that therefore whites and blacks have a common interest in opposing apartheid. Such an analysis distorts the question of power. There are whites in power who benefit from the system and work actively or passively to preserve it. Without organization and struggle, the blacks are powerless to oppose it. Liberalism stands aloof from power questions and therefore functions to maintain the status quo. The Maoist ethic puts the question of power at the center of its analysis by asking which classes and groups benefit from the unjust system and how they can be overthrown.

The liberal will say that Maoism leads to violence and disorder. As Merleau-Ponty has written, however, the liberal humanist system of the West is also a violent war machine.[8] It uses police and the army to maintain the violence of unemployment, colonial wars, and economic inequality. The people of the Third World, he wrote, have seen "a lot of our arms but not much of our humanism." In its own eyes, "Western humanism appears as the love of humanity," but in the eyes of others it is the privileged possession of a small group that preserves its interests by violence.[9] "Revolutions," wrote Merleau-Ponty, "taken altogether have not spilled as much blood as the empires."[10]

China's experience with the West would confirm Merleau-Ponty's view of the violence of the systems in which liberalism flourishes. Opium wars, gunboat diplomacy, economic manipulation, unequal treaties, semicolonial control are what China experienced at the hands of the same nations from which it learned about liberalism and humanism. It is no wonder the lessons about liberal values were not very convincing.

To sum up, China's revolutionaries reject liberalism because it is a world view which functions within the limits of the privileged class, though expressing its values in universal terms. Liberalism also creates a facade of peace and harmony rather than confronting real conflicts in society. By seeking to stand above conflicts, liberalism functions to preserve unjust situations. As a world view it does not deal realistically with power and the struggle for justice. China suffered many injustices at the hands of the Western liberal democracies, which only strengthened its rejection of liberalism.

Human nature and class struggle. In the West we often use the phrase "it's only human nature" to explain or excuse various forms of behavior. It is only human nature to want to get ahead; to want privilege, wealth, and prestige; to make mistakes; to place personal survival and gain in a primary position. Popular statements about human nature reflect the predominant liberal philosophy of the West. This liberal view is based on the classical and Judeo-Christian concepts of sin and pride. The original goodness of human beings has been distorted by pride, greed, and other forms of self-centeredness or sin. In liberalism, provision is made for these defects in human nature. It is necessary, in the liberal view, to have a system where people can achieve personal rewards for their individual efforts. Each person struggles greedily against all others for a larger share of society's resources, because this is human nature.

Capitalism makes a virtue out of this greed. Since it is human nature to want to gain more for self, then the best system is the free marketplace where all can work, invest, start business enterprises, push ahead through diligence and wit. In this theory, greater good will accrue to the whole community through the competitive spirit of each against all. People are rewarded with greater wealth for their enterprising spirit. The desire for these rewards will motivate everyone to harder work and greater creativity, resulting in more goods for the whole society. There will be economic inequality, but even those at the bottom will benefit from the bigger pie that such a system creates.

The Maoists reject this understanding of human nature. (In doing so they say that there is no human essence common to all persons. Maoist thought is inconsistent at this point, an issue that will be discussed below.) The grounds for rejection of the bourgeois theory of human nature are (1) by ignoring class distinctions it is artificial and abstract, (2) it is too individualistic, (3) it camouflages oppression by glossing over class differences, (4) it is deceptive in its use of universal formulations, and (5) it confuses the questions of power and struggle.

The central point of Mao's thought and ethic is class struggle. The liberal view of human nature, and the liberal values in general, use formulations that ignore class struggle. The liberal view is that human nature is inborn. This essential human nature is the same for every person. The Maoists say that in class societies (which means all societies now in existence—there are as yet no classless societies, not even in communist countries) a person is born into a particular class and develops the "nature" of that class. The liberal view is "abstract," say the Maoists, because it talks about a human nature separate from any particular person or any particular social group. In the words of Mao:

Is there such a thing as human nature? Of course there is. But there is only human nature in the concrete, no human nature in the abstract. In a class society there is only human nature of a class character; there is no human nature above classes. We uphold the human nature of the proletariat and of the masses of the people, while the landlord and bourgeois classes uphold the human nature of their own classes, only they do not say so but make it out to be the only human nature in existence. The human nature boosted by certain petty-bourgeois intellectuals is also divorced from or opposed to the masses; what they call human nature is contrary to human nature.[11]

To support this view Maoist writers quote Karl Marx: "But the essence of man is no abstraction inherent in each separate individual. In its reality it is the ensemble (aggregate) of social relations."[12] The Maoists take this to mean that class character and human nature are identical. There is no abstract human nature possessed equally by the exploiter and the exploited, the master and the slave.

According to Maoist interpretations the radical thrust of Marx's thinking is in his refusal to analyze problems from the point of view of some universal theory of human nature. Instead they see Marx as linking human nature and class struggle. Human nature is not innate. It is related to economic status. There is no human encounter in some ethereal realm divorced from class position. All social relations are branded with the class character of the persons entering into such relations.[13] The only way human encounter can occur un-colored by class relations will be in the future classless society. There is a common humanity but it will be realized only in a time yet to come.

The Maoists also find individualistic aspects of the bourgeois theory of human nature to be inconsistent with their under-standing of Marxism. The liberal bourgeois attitude had ex-tensive influence among intellectuals in China, who often op-posed Maoist views on the grounds that they went against human nature. Some infellectuals said that any discipline that conflicted with personal desires was a violation of the freedom of personality.

The Maoist response to such individualistic views of human nature is that these views cover over an underlying selfishness. Such views undermine collective spirit and identification with workers and peasants. Freedom of personality, according to the Maoists, is an issue which cannot be separated from the question of class and class struggle. Intellectuals are charged with using concepts of human nature and personality to avoid struggle, the issue of justice, and the question of whom one serves.

The appeal to human nature and freedom of personality is not just an academic, philosophical point, according to the Maoists, but a basic social question of how the life of workers and peasants is related to that of intellectuals and scholars. To insist, on the basis of the human nature theory, that intellectuals must be free to develop their personalities and creativity unhindered, is to disguise the selfish desire to preserve privileged positions. Personal development has to be sought in the context of a community where workers and peasants have equal dignity with scholars and intellectuals. If not, then the human nature theory is simply functioning to preserve unjust class distinctions.[14]

The Maoists are not satisfied with the liberal view of human nature because it, like other liberal values, places every person in the same situation. If emphasis is put on the common human nature shared by peasant and landlord, worker and capitalist, slave and slaveholder, then revolutionary resolve is diluted—all are in the same boat confronting common human problems. Such a dilution of revolutionary resolve only serves the interests of those who are benefitting from the unjust system. It is no help to the peasant, worker, or slave to be indoctrinated with the idea of common human nature. It only confuses the question of who is the enemy.

Some Marxist writers in China were criticized for distorting this problem. One theoretician attempted to write a philosophy that would serve "mankind in general." He wrote about the common characteristics of all persons. It is the nature of men, he said, to seek happiness and avoid harm. Man's happiness will increase with the increase of production. He saw class struggle as a "great artificial catastrophe." Social contradictions were not important in his view.

Maoist critics of this writer said that in trying to set out a philosophy that would serve humankind he ended up with one that served only the interests of the bourgeoisie. In writing about common human nature he negated class contradictions and abolished class struggle. He took as basic the problem of how humanity deals with technological development and not how the oppressed carry out revolution.[15] From the Maoist point of view he fell into the trap of the human nature theory. He reduced the problem to the common effort of humankind to achieve development. In doing this he clouded the problem of the struggle for equality and justice. In the Maoist view, all people are not in the same boat. Or if they are, a few are going first class. The majority are chained to the oars.

The liberal view of human nature is a deception, say the Maoists. It hides the realities of privilege and exploitation. This is not to say that exploitation is the only problem. Development and increased production are necessary. Development goals, however, do not clash with social goals. Development will come about most quickly if the initiative of the whole population is brought into play. This will happen only if the workers and peasants are actively involved in the development process. If production goals are given exclusive attention, then there is a tendency for power to gravitate into the hands of a small group of technological experts. These experts become a new class who support various versions of the liberal view of human nature because it de-emphasizes the question of justice and gives all attention to the common human problem of technological development. The revolution is then set back because the workers and peasants are made passive followers of the new class of experts. This undermines both development goals, because workers and peasants are put in a passive position, and revolutionary goals, because a new set of class distinctions is introduced.[16]

The above scenario represents what the Maoists understand to be happening in the Soviet Union. The liberal view of human nature finds a new home in the camp of Soviet revisionism. Revisionism neglects class struggle. The Russians falsely assume that classes have been eliminated in their country. The central issue for them is no longer class contradiction and the struggle for justice, but the problem of production. This is a deception, say the Maoists, because class contradictions continue in socialist societies, including Russia and China. To live by the illusion that classes have been eliminated only plays into the hands of those who are wielding power unfairly for their own personal benefit. Liberalism and revisionism are twins, according to the Maoists. Their theories of human nature, beneath all the rhetoric, are identical.

Those who support a class-transcending view of human

nature do not clearly perceive the power struggle taking place in society. One historian claimed, for example, that in imperial China there was a common interest between the landlords and the peasants and that the state machinery represented "the whole people." The Maoists say that this is not true, and that such a view of history is misleading for peasants today. If peasants think they have a common nature and a common interest with landlords then they will have an unrealistic view of the power that exploits them. It is an illusion to assume that exploiters will voluntarily lay down their butcher knives and become Buddhas, say the Maoists.

Just as it is not true historically that landlords and peasants had a common interest that overrode their class struggle, so also in China's socialist society today revolution has not ended. Class struggle still continues. Those who downplay the class struggle of the past also wish to hide the issues of power and struggle today.[17] The liberal view of human nature reappears in Marxist garb, but it still functions to protect the power of a privileged stratum.[18]

The Maoist position, to summarize, rejects the liberal bourgeois theory of human nature on theoretical grounds and because of its social consequences. The human nature theory is abstracted from the context of social class, it is over-individualistic, it disguises class oppression, it is illusory and deceptive, and it beclouds issues of power and struggle.

In opposing the bourgeois theory of human nature the Maoists go to the extreme of saying that there is no common nature shared by all individual persons. Although the theoretical and social grounds for their argument are quite convincing, the Maoist position is, nevertheless, involved in a logical inconsistency, as we have already mentioned.

The Maoist position is that there is no common ground, no common interest, no common human nature between the oppressed and the oppressors. In a class society human nature means class nature. Since there are different classes there are different human natures. The human nature of the proletariat is different from the human nature of the bourgeoisie. Those who speak of a common human nature that is a given for each human being regardless of class undermine revolutionary class struggle.

There are three aspects of Mao's thought that seem logically inconsistent with this position on human nature. First, the Maoists speak of the need for the liberation of all humankind and look forward to a future classless society when human nature and class nature will be common to all persons. If there is the prospect of such a universal human nature in the future does this not imply that all persons now have something in common that makes them potential candidates for the future classless society?

Second, we have seen that the Maoists believe it is possible for people to change their class stand. A bourgeois person can become a proletarian and a worker or peasant can be corrupted by bourgeois attitudes.[19] If it is possible to move from one class to another, does this not imply that the persons who are part of different classes share some basic common humanity?

Third, Mao's thought itself uses universal formulations. The theory of contradictions is that every phenomenon is characterized by the struggle of opposing forces. Does this not imply that at least a common contradictory nature is shared by all human beings? One could say, by implication, on the basis of Mao's writings, that thought struggle is a part of the human nature of all persons.

I am entirely sympathetic with the Maoist attempt to expose the use of the liberal theory of human nature to thwart the struggle for justice. In taking the extreme position that there is no human nature apart from class nature, however, the Maoists have involved themselves in a logical inconsistency. What is necessary, it would seem, is for Maoist philosophers to develop a theory of human nature that (1) is based on the struggle ethic and the theory of contradictions, (2) clearly excludes the misuses of the liberal theory of human nature, and (3) provides a logical place for the three aspects of Mao's thought mentioned above.

Equality, freedom, and love. If we understand why liberalism and the liberal view of human nature are rejected by the

Maoists (even if we do not agree), then we are in a position to try to comprehend their even more scandalous rejection of liberal values such as equality, freedom, and love. How can anyone be against love!

The motto of the French Revolution, "liberty, equality, fraternity," is frequently criticized in Maoist writings. "Fraternity" is translated into Chinese as *bo ai,* broad or universal love. In rejecting this motto the Chinese Marxists would appear to be against freedom, love, and equality.

Maoists contend that liberty-equality-fraternity is a motto that was revolutionary at the time of the struggle of the rising bourgeoisie against the old feudal order. In the present period this slogan has lost its revolutionary quality. The bourgeoisie now use the values of liberty-equality-fraternity in a deceitful way to resist the proletarian revolution.[20]

How can liberty-equality-fraternity be used to resist the proletariat's struggle for justice? This is done by abstracting the slogan from the concrete conditions of class struggle. Lenin, say the Maoists, saw as the most diabolical enemies those who took liberty-equality-fraternity as a slogan unrelated to class struggle.[21]

In the American tradition it is taken as a self-evident truth that all persons are created equal. At the time of Thomas Jefferson this phrase was revolutionary. It declared an equality of commoner with king. Even then, however, this equality did not extend to slaves, women, or native American Indians. The gap between words and practice is an aspect of the liberal view of equality that Maoists criticize.

The liberal view has continued to preserve basic inequality while speaking in terms of equality, according to the Maoist view. Those with wealth and power in Western societies talk about equality: Everyone has the right to vote, all are equal before the law, and all have equal right to pursue their own interests. The Maoists say that this equality is a hoax. Factory workers and farm hands do not have equal access to the media to express their views. Wealthy people have much more to say about who the candidates in any election will be. The poor suffer more under the legal system than those with friends in high places or with the means to hire good lawyers. The Maoists feel that in China as well those who use equality as a slogan, without reference to class struggle, are usually those who are in comfortable positions that they wish to protect.[22]

The liberal view of freedom or liberty is also rejected by the Maoists because it does not deal with the realities of class struggle. To say that the capitalist is "free" to buy labor power and that the worker is "free" to sell labor power is to abuse the word "free." This labor system, say the Maoists, is simply slavery of a more subtle form.[23] The political freedom shared by both the super-rich capitalist and the struggling farm worker, for example, does not alleviate the essential economic disparity between the two. Political freedom needs to be evaluated in light of the economic situation. Wealth gives the capitalist a whole range of freedoms (access to travel, culture, education, health care, safe housing, ample food) that poverty denies the farm worker. In reality the capitalist and the farm worker are involved in a class conflict. Any concept of freedom that ignores this class struggle distorts one's perception of reality.

In China after liberation, say the Maoists, it is those capitalist roaders who have control of educational facilities and the media who are the first to speak about freedom. They do not give the workers and peasants free access to these facilities. The capitalist roaders talk about freedom of speech but really use this as a cover to protect their own special privilege. They say they want freedom of speech but they do not want to hear about continuing class struggle in a socialist society because this will threaten their comfortable positions.[24]

In the slogan liberty-equality-fraternity the third term, we have said, is translated into Chinese as "universal love." This means that when the term is translated into English from Chinese sources it sometimes appears as "fraternity" and sometimes as "love." The Maoists see love also in relation to class struggle.

Mao Zedong, speaking about literature and art, refuted the

claims of those who said that the fundamental point of departure for the writer or artist was "love of humanity." Mao countered:

Now love may serve as a point of departure, but there is a more basic one. Love as an idea is a product of objective practice. Fundamentally, we do not start from ideas but from objective practice. Our writers and artists who come from the ranks of the intellectuals love the proletariat because society made them feel that they and the proletariat share a common fate. We hate Japanese imperialism because Japanese imperialism oppresses us. There is absolutely no such thing in the world as love or hatred without reason or cause. As for the so-called love of humanity, there has been no such all inclusive love since humanity was divided into classes. All the ruling classes of the past were fond of advocating it, and so were many so-called sages and wise men, but nobody has ever really practiced it, because it is impossible in a class society. There will be genuine love of humanity—after classes are eliminated all over the world. Classes have split society into many antagonistic groupings; there will be love of all humanity when classes are eliminated, but not now. We cannot love enemies, we cannot love social evils, our aim is to destroy them. This is common sense; can it be that some of our writers and artists still do not understand this?[25]

Mao's point here is that since society is divided into classes it is not possible to work realistically on the principle of a universal love which ignores class distinctions.

Love of humanity is rejected because it uses universal formulation while in fact supporting an exploitative system.[26] Those with wealth and power will not think in terms of class struggle. For them, love of humanity is a very useful concept. If those who are oppressed are taught to love all persons equally, then the rulers will be seen by the oppressed primarily as fellow human beings to be loved. Those in power would much rather see class distinctions thus overlooked and emphasis put on human love.

The liberal values of liberty, equality, and fraternity (and related values such as humanism, humanitarianism, and pacifism) are seen by the Maoists as supporting an exploitative system because they confuse the problem of class struggle.[27]

The Maoists see these concepts as smoke screens created by bourgeois or revisionist groups who want to divert attention from class struggle and from their own positions of privilege, wealth, and power.

The Maoists also find love, equality, freedom to be absent in those societies that talk so much about them. The words "love of humanity" are used by exploitative groups to make palatable the colonial wars, oppression, and plunder they practice. Words of love are spoken, but what is done represents simply "civilized selfishness."[28]

Within the People's Republic of China there are also some who support the values of liberty-equality-fraternity. Those who do are not the workers and peasants, but rather cadres and intellectuals in privileged positions, according to Maoist critics. Since, in Mao's view, class struggle continues even in a socialist society, it is necessary to analyze the motives of those who push aside the question of class and appeal to love, freedom, and equality. These words are used by the capitalist roaders in China in the same way as they are used by the bourgeoisie in the West. At one and the same time, they use the slogan liberty-equality-fraternity and treat workers and peasants with contempt; they do not allow common people equal opportunity to express their views.[29]

During the Cultural Revolution, for example, it was revealed that in postsecondary institutions the vast majority of students were from cadre and former bourgeois families. There were entrance examinations which supposedly gave every student equal opportunity to enroll. In fact, however, the system functioned in such a way that children of workers and peasants were largely excluded. Those who were trying to preserve this unfair system did so in the name of equality and freedom. They did not wish to face the class distinctions preserved by the developing system or admit that class struggle was continuing in China.

It is very important in seeking to understand the Maoist position to realize that in rejecting the "bourgeois slogan" of liberty-equality-fraternity, Maoists are not opposing freedom, egalitarianism, and love. What they are denying is that these values are meaningful apart from a consistent analysis of class and class struggle. If class struggle is left out, then the expressed values are negated in practice. The values of those who are benefitting unequally from the system will almost always be stated in terms of the common good. The struggle of the oppressed will be played down by speaking about the human problems faced by all of us together.

The rejection of liberty-equality-fraternity by Mao does not mean an affirmation of slavery, inequality, and cruelty. It is true that Maoists treat reactionaries and exploiters with "inequality" under the "dictatorship of the proletariat."[30] That is to say, workers and peasants have attained power and have put limits on those who want to live by exploiting others. Equality does not mean that each person has the equal right to seek as much money and power as he or she can attain from the sweat of others.

Egalitarianism is emphasized in China even though the liberal view of equality is rejected. There is equality among the people. The resources of society are distributed fairly, by and large. Dignity is given to all kinds of work. Leaders are admonished to stay close to the masses and to treat the common people on an "equal footing."[31] All people are expected to take part in physical labor and all have access to educational and cultural resources.

The rejection of the bourgeois view of liberty does not mean that Mao supports slavery. The question of liberty or freedom also has a class dimension. The revolution in China has placed limits on certain kinds of freedom. There is no freedom to exploit, say the Maoists, nor to resist socialism. "If we want to be free from oppression and the menace of imperialism, there cannot be freedom for imperialism . . . aggression, [and] oppression."[32]

Although the bourgeois slogan about freedom has been opposed, liberty and liberation through class struggle has been affirmed. The majority of the people at the basic level have greatly increased freedom to participate in the process of decision-making on issues that immediately affect their lives. The economic status of the masses, which drastically limited their personal freedom prior to the revolution, has been dramatically altered. If freedom is considered in terms of access to the benefits of society—adequate food and shelter, health care, education, cultural life—then the net gain in personal freedom for the majority of Chinese is obvious.

Rejection of the liberal view of fraternity or love also does not mean the rejection of love as such. Love and self-sacrifice play important and positive roles when seen from the perspective of class struggle. In "Serve the People," Mao writes that concern must be shown for everyone involved in the struggle and that "all people in the revolutionary ranks must care for each other, must love and help each other."[33]

When Norman Bethune, the Canadian doctor, gave his life serving the people's army in the war against Japan, Mao commended his "great warmheartedness" and selfless devotion and urged others to learn from his spirit of dedication.[34] Loving and serving the people are central values in Mao's ethical thought, but only when put in the context of class struggle.

Mao's thought does not reject love for the sake of hatred but for the sake of justice. There is a positive emphasis on hatred of the enemy in his ethic, however, that may be called "creative animosity." The enemy is to be hated and destroyed. This does not mean killing all the members of the enemy class, but destroying their power to exploit and enslave. When the power of enemies has been broken they can be dealt with "on the basis of equality and mutual benefit" and transformed into useful citizens.[35]

Animosity, according to Mao, animates oppressed people to resist oppression and to struggle. The opposite of hatred of the enemy is seen not as love but as slavishness. For oppressed people to love their oppressors means, according to Mao, a reduction in the will of the oppressed to carry out revolution. It is necessary to make a distinction between friends and enemies, to unite with the former to attack the latter.[36] When the oppressors have been overthrown, then the situation of class antagonism, which prevented genuine love, is changed. Love is possible after the victory of the revolutionary struggle against the class enemies who created the original situation of oppression and animosity. The question of love cannot be separated from issues of power and justice.

To sum up, the Maoist critique of liberty-equality-fraternity is based on the ethic of class struggle. The oppressed and downtrodden do not share in the liberty and equality enjoyed by the bourgeoisie. The liberal values are expressed in universal terms but do not exist universally. These values distort class analysis and struggle by framing issues in terms of "mankind." The rejection of liberty-equality-fraternity is not for the sake of slavery, inequality, and cruelty.

Out of Mao's own writings it would be possible to reinterpret these liberal values as "liberation, classless society, serving of the people." In Mao's ethic there is emphasis on freedom as liberation, on equality as the classless society, and on fraternity as serving the people. The underlying thrust of the liberal values is affirmed in Mao's "revolutionary humanism," but the distortion of these values, which comes from ignoring class struggle and power questions, is exposed.

The liberal view of truth. The liberal view of truth is captured in the popular phrase "free marketplace of ideas." Presumably the liberal academic atmosphere is one of the marketplace, where all ideas can be freely expressed and exchanged. Ideological prejudices are frowned upon. Each person enters the marketplace with only his or her critical capabilities. Through objective study and consideration truth can be apprehended by the open-minded individual.

From the Maoist point of view the free marketplace of ideas is a fraud. It is a commercial image that appeals to the bourgeois mind, but the marketplace of ideas is not free. Individuals do not come to it with an objectivity uninfluenced by class background. The marketplace of ideas is not freely accessible to people from lower-class backgrounds. Like other markets, it is subject to manipulation and utilization by those with power. The question of truth, like the questions of love and liberty, cannot be approached in isolation from problems of power, social practice, and class struggle.

The Maoist position is that truth has a class character. There are some problems in this Maoist position. It is not clarified in Maoist writings whether truth itself has a class character or whether it is the perception of truth that is influenced by class. The following passage indicates this problem:

Don't you know that there is only class truth in class society and no such thing as abstract truth above classes? Different classes always hold different views on what is truth and what is falsehood. Truth is objective. There can be only one truth, and who after all arrives at the truth depends . . . on objective practice. The only criterion of truth is the revolutionary practice of the millions of people. Only the proletariat, which is the most advanced and most revolutionary class, can understand the objective laws of social development and grasp the truth.[37]

It is stated here both that truth is objective and that there is only class truth.

The central point of the Maoist position, in contrast with the liberal view, is that truth about social and political questions cannot be grasped apart from class struggle. In seeking truth the struggle ethic remains basic. It is necessary to be involved in class struggle, to stand on the side of the dispossessed, in order to find revolutionary truth. The Maoist image is not one of humanity seeking truth, but of the oppressed seeking justice. The search for truth is intimately related to the struggle for justice. Even to proclaim to be a follower of Mao's thought, apart from participation in struggle on the side of the common people, does not give one any special claims on revolutionary truth.

University communities in the West usually see themselves as groups of people seeking objective truth and not involved in class struggle. There is the same tendency in China. Academic authorities do not like to confront the question of whether or not the university system is giving rise to a new class of privileged scholars. When challenged their response is that these are "matters of academic discussion" within the university. They call for "calm and constructive" discussion of the issues.

The Maoist answer is that all learning is influenced by class interests, and that there cannot be any construction of a new just society without the destruction of special privilege.[38]

Rather than face the issue of class struggle university professors raise the slogan "everyone is equal before the truth." Again, the Maoists see this as a way of muddying the waters. To say that everyone is equal before the truth puts the problem in terms of humankind facing error. This overlooks the class struggle going on within humankind and shields the scholars from the necessity of taking a stand in the struggle for justice. They see themselves simply as human beings seeking truth. For the Maoists, individuals are not just human beings in the abstract. Each person lives in a social context and must seek truth while participating in the specific historical struggle of the oppressed. The enemy is not human error primarily, but groups and classes who wield power unjustly. Therefore the slogan "everyone equal before the truth" must be resisted.[39]

How is truth to be discovered then? According to Mao, truth (or "correct ideas") does not "drop from the skies" like some kind of revelation, nor is it innate in the mind. Correct ideas are discovered in social practice—the struggle for production, scientific experiment, and class struggle.[40]

On the question of scientific and technological truth the Maoist position is unclear. If the perception of truth is always influenced by class, then is scientific truth also more accessible to the proletarian than to the bourgeois? This is clearly an untenable position. The Maoist would say, at least, that the life of the scientist is related to class struggle. No one stands outside some social context. Scientists and technologists who assume that their knowledge places them above the common people and the struggle for justice are in error and are in danger of becoming enemies of the people.

Is there any way to verify the truth of Mao's thought in the area of social and political revolution? Mao has written that sometimes oppressed people suffer defeat in their revolutionary struggle not because their ideas are wrong but because the power of the oppressors is too great. Mao sees such defeat as temporary. He is convinced that revolutionary struggle will eventually be successful.[41] One failure or one success is not final verification of the truth or error of a particular revolutionary movement.

In seeking revolutionary truth the measurement of success and failure is itself very difficult. If we take the Chinese revolution as an example, there are many different opinions about whether it has been successful or not, or to what degree. How can one prove the success of Mao's revolution and verify the truth of his thought?

This way of phrasing the question reflects the basic problem of liberal and Maoist views of truth. I have raised the question in its liberal form: How can we objectively prove the validity of Mao's thought? The Maoists would say, prove it for whom —the bourgeoisie or the workers and peasants? If the perception of truth is influenced by class then there can be no way of validating the truth of Mao's thought in supraclass categories. Those opposed to the revolutionary struggle of the oppressed will of course not be able to perceive the truth of Mao's thought.

The Maoist position on the class nature of truth puts an end to discussion. If we Western liberals are prevented by our class background from perceiving revolutionary truth, then it is impossible to "understand" Mao and the Chinese revolution. As with the question of human nature, so with the question of truth, the Maoist position is not totally consistent. Maoists do try to communicate the truth, as they see it, to all kinds of people from various backgrounds. In the United Nations, in world conferences on such problems as food, population, and the law of the sea, the Chinese representatives have stated positions that they obviously hope will be intelligible even to Western, bourgeois liberals. If truth were totally determined by class perception, then such communication would be impossible.

There are three areas where the Chinese position on the question of truth seems inconsistent, even on their own grounds. The point just discussed is that if perception of truth is totally determined by class, then communication across class lines would be impossible. Yet the Maoists do attempt just such communication.

Second, it was mentioned above that Maoists seem inconsistent on the issue of the perception of scientific truth. Water boils at 100° C. regardless of class background. The Maoists seem ready to accept and utilize scientific truth that comes from bourgeois liberal scholars, without fear that this truth has been distorted by the class background of the scientists.

Third, there is an inconsistency on whether or not it is truth or the perception of truth that is determined by class. Maoists seem to come down on the side of class-influenced perception rather than class-influenced truth. Even though the Maoists say that in a class society there is only class truth, they also universalize their own view of truth. The proletariat is seen as the only class in history "whose own liberation is based on the universal liberation of mankind and whose revolutionary principles are truly the revolutionary principles of all the people."[42] Here truth is spoken of in terms of humankind and all the people.

In spite of these problems and inconsistencies it is possible to appreciate the Maoist position on the class nature of truth. Much that passes for objective truth in the academic world is simply a defense of the injustices of the system. The search for truth is not a process that takes place in an abstract "free marketplace of ideas" but is one which is very much influenced by questions of class background and the power of various groups represented in the process. The basic thrust of the Maoist view of truth is very useful although the position is often overstated, leading to logical inconsistencies.

Conclusion

In previous chapters we looked at the background and development of Mao's thought and ethic and how this ethic works out in the transformation of society, persons, and lifestyle. Underlying all this discussion was the question of the conflict between the Maoist world view and ethic on the one hand and the bourgeois liberal view on the other. The liberal world view is that which underlies Western thought in general, so the conflict has been between our Western world view and the Maoist world view.

In this chapter we have been looking at this conflict of world views and values in greater detail. Of the various elements of the liberal world view we chose liberalism, the theory of human nature, liberty-equality-fraternity, and the liberal view of truth, to see what were the features of this conflict.

In all these elements of the liberal world view there is a tendency to formulate problems in terms of humankind facing certain issues. There is struggle involved in the liberal world view and ethic, but it is the struggle of humankind against inhumanity, narrow-mindedness, sin and pride, nature, underdevelopment, tyranny, inequality, hatred, ignorance, and error.

The Maoists reject the liberal world view and the ideas of objectivity, human nature, love, freedom, equality, and truth, which we in the West consider to be noble and sacred values. At first glance we can only ask how it is possible to come to appreciate Mao's thought when it rejects the values we hold dear.

I have attempted to show that in the Maoist view these values are not rejected in the name of slavery and inequality and hatred and falsehood. The liberal values are rejected because, from the Maoist standpoint, they do not exist in the societies that proclaim them. The very use of these values in liberal thought is for the purpose of hiding the real problems of society.

The liberal approach sees values such as equality and freedom in legal terms, but ignores the economic dimension. The rich and the poor are not equal, say the Maoists, even though they may have legal equality. Someone with great wealth has all kinds of "freedom" not enjoyed by the person who is struggling for a mere existence.

From the Maoist point of view these economic differences, these class differences, are of overwhelming importance. In all societies today there is conflict between those with wealth and power and those who are poor and powerless. Ignoring this class struggle, high-sounding liberal values simply support injustice.

In the Maoist ethic there is a concern for humanity, the liberation of all humankind. The rejection of liberal humanism is not a rejection of humanity but a recognition that the division of society into struggling classes prevents an expression of true humanity. Our common humanity is in the future, the classless society. The struggle ethic of Mao claims it is necessary to work to overcome the inhumanity of class oppression. The liberal error is that the existence of a common humanity is presupposed. Liberalism thus camouflages the class struggle taking place in society.

The struggle ethic of Mao constantly raises the question of class differences and the inhumanity that such differences create. Maoists go to the extreme of denying any common humanity and any truth apart from class, which involves them in logical inconsistencies. This weakness of the Maoist position does not negate its usefulness in exposing the way liberal values profess one thing while supporting another.

I have raised the problem we face as bourgeois liberals in dealing with an ethic and world view that reject liberalism. The Maoist ethic rejects liberal values, allows for violent struggle against those who use violence to oppress the people, demands commitment and the taking of a stand on the side of the people, encourages creative animosity, and gives a central place to class struggle. How do we respond to Mao's ethic and world view when it stands in such contrast to our own?

I have tried to show how the rejection of liberal values such as love, freedom, and tolerance for the weaknesses of human nature does not mean a rejection of human concern, but of the false use of "human values" to support their opposite. In the Maoist ethic there is concern for human liberation, for love and mutuality among the revolutionary people, for breaking down the class distinctions of power and wealth, and for arriving at truth or correct ideas through social practice.

As a Western liberal, then, I find my humanistic values challenged by Mao's ethic. This is not a challenge resulting from "Maoist inhumanity," as some of us may have believed in the past, but a challenge to the inhumanity buried within our stated humanism. As Merleau-Ponty said, the people of the world have suffered a great deal from the armaments of Western, liberal, humanist nations, and have seen little of our humanism and love.

The struggle ethic of Mao confronts us with serious questions about our values and ethics. It asks us where we stand in relation to class struggle, in relation to the oppressed of the world. It asks whom it is that we serve in our life and work. It asks whose side we are on. It asks whom we see as the enemies of the people and whether or not we are living lives of struggle and frugality and service to the people. In rejecting the liberal world view it raises the very issues with which our liberalism professes to be concerned.

NOTES

1. Robert J. Lifton, *Thought Reform and the Psychology of Totalism* (London: Victor Gollancz, 1962), pp. 378–87.

2. SW II, pp. 31–33.

3. Erich Fromm, *Marx's Concept of Man* (New York: Frederick Ungar, 1961), pp. ix–x.

4. Ibid., pp. 46–50, 68.

5. C. Wright Mills, *The Marxists* (Harmondsworth: Penguin Books, 1963), pp. 26–28.

6. Ibid., pp. 28–31.

7. Ibid., pp. 110–11.

8. Maurice Merleau-Ponty, *Humanism and Terror,* tr. John O'Neill (Boston: Beacon Press, 1969), p. 186. The original French edition was published in 1947.

9. Ibid., pp. 175–76.

10. Ibid., p. 107.

11. SW III, p. 90.

12. Quoted in Han Chia-ch'en, "On the Essential Nature of Man," *PD,* December 8, 1962, SCMP, no. 2888 (December 31, 1962), pp. 1–4.

13. Ibid., pp. 3–4.

14. Wang Tzu-yeh, "Hu Feng's 'On Human Nature' Just a Lie," *CY,* no. 18 (1955), ECMM, no. 15 (November 21, 1955), pp. 7–8.

15. The theoretician criticized by the Maoists is Feng Ting. His books, *The Communist View of Life* and *Commonplace Truth,* had numerous printings in

various editions in the late 1950s and early 1960s. They were distributed widely for use in the education of young people. See Lu Feng, "A Big Hotchpotch of Subjective Idealism: A Comment on Comrade Feng Ting's *Commonplace Truth*," *RF,* nos. 21–22 (November 21, 1964, double issue), SCMM, no. 447 (December 14, 1964), pp. 1, 5–10.

16. See also John Gurley, "Maoist Economic Development: The New Man in the New China," *The Center Magazine,* May 1970.

17. Mass Criticism Group of Hopei Normal College (authors), "Firmly Uphold Class Struggle, Oppose Class Conciliation," KM, January 15, 1971, SCMP, no. 4830 (February 3, 1971), pp. 74–81.

18. Ting Hsueh-li, "Criticize and Repudiate Liu Shao-ch'i's Reactionary Theory of Human Nature," RF, no. 11 (October 1, 1971), SCMM, no. 716 (November 8, 1971), pp. 45–57.

19. Mao wrote: "Whoever sides with the revolutionary people is a revolutionary. Whoever sides with imperialism, feudalism and bureaucratic capitalism is a counter-revolutionary. Whoever sides with the revolutionary people in words only but acts otherwise is a revolutionary in speech. Whoever sides with the revolutionary people in deed as well as in word is a revolutionary in the full sense" (*Quotations from Chairman Mao Tse-tung* [Peking: Foreign Languages Press, 1966], p. 14).

20. Sa Jen-hsing, " 'Liberty, Equality, and Fraternity' and the Proletarian Dictatorship," *Philosophical Research,* no. 1 (January 10, 1960), ECMM, no. 211 (May 16, 1960), pp. 16–18. (Sa Jen-hsing is a pseudonym for Kuan Feng. He was criticized in the Cultural Revolution.)

21. Ibid.

22. Wang Ching-cheng, "On Egalitarianism," *Study,* no. 101 (November 2, 1956), ECMM, no. 67 (January 28, 1957), p. 7.

23. Li Ch'ing-t'ien and Chao Yi-min, "Humanism Is a Product of Capitalist Relationship," *Philosophical Research,* no. 3 (May 25, 1964), SCMM, no. 427 (July 23, 1964), pp. 28–33.

24. Editorial, "Tear Aside the Bourgeois Mask of 'Liberty, Equality and Fraternity,' " *PD,* June 1966, English translation in *The Great Cultural Revolution in China* (Hong Kong: Asia Research Centre, 1967), pp. 271–72.

25. SW III, pp. 90–91.

26. Wu Chiang, "A Discourse on Public Interests and Individual Interests," CY, nos. 23–24 (December 10, 1961), SCMM, no. 297 (January 22, 1962), p. 2.

27. See Cheng Chih, "Learn From Lei Feng, Increase Consciousness in Ideological Remoulding," CY, no. 9 (May 1, 1963), SCMM, no. 371 (July 2, 1963), pp. 15–19, and Li Ch'ing-t'ien and Chao Yi-min, "Humanism is a Product of Capitalist Relationship," *Philosophical Research,* no. 3 (May 25, 1964), SCMM, no. 427 (July 23, 1964), pp. 28–33, which includes the following passage:

> We hold that humanism is the world outlook of the bourgeoisie, another way to preach the "liberty, equality, and fraternity" of the bourgeoisie, and also a name to prettify bourgeois individualism. It is a product of capitalist relationships, and an ideological weapon to consolidate capitalist relationships. Humanism was never something known in the old feudal society.

Humanism is a kind of phenomenon of social consciousness. Consciousness is determined by existence, and a certain consciousness can only be explained with [reference to] the existence of a certain economy. The humanists worship abstract man, and their idea of the isolation of individuals, their abstract "liberty" and "equality" and their abstract "love," all reflect the capitalist commodity relationship.

To the humanists, "man" is a kind of "man" pure and abstract. In actuality, he is a property owner. However, this kind of metaphysical and abstract idea of "man" of theirs owes its origin to modern bourgeois society in which all kinds of relationships are in actuality subordinate to the abstract relationship of money and exploitation. It goes without saying that this kind of metaphysical and abstract idea of "man" cannot have occurred in the relationships of feudal production in ancient times.

28. Wu Chiang, "A Discourse on Public Interests and Individual Interests," CY, nos. 23–24 (December 10, 1961), SCMM, no. 297 (January 22, 1962), p. 2.

29. *The Great Cultural Revolution in China*, pp. 271–74.

30. Sa Jen-hsing, " 'Liberty, Equality and Fraternity' and the Proletarian Dictatorship," *Philosophical Research*, no. 1 (January 10, 1960), SCMM, no. 211 (May 16, 1960), pp. 16–18.

31. Ibid.

32. Ibid.

33. SW III, p. 178.

34. SW II, pp. 337–38.

35. SW IV, p. 429.

36. SW I, p. 13.

37. *The Great Cultural Revolution in China*, p. 273. See also the editorial "Long Live the Great Revolution of the Proletariat," RF, no. 8 (1966), SCMM, no. 530 (June 27, 1966), p. 9, where it is stated: "Truth has a class character. In the contemporary era, only the proletariat can grasp objective truth because its class interests are one with objective law. The reactionary and corrupt bourgeoisie has long been isolated from the truth and its so-called "truth" can only be a fallacy that runs counter to the current of the times and objective law."

38. "Long Live the Great Revolution of the Proletariat," p. 7.

39. "Can 'everyone be equal' before the truth? We answer: 'No! No! No!' Truth has a class character" (In the editorial "Refuting the Bourgeois Slogan, 'Everyone Is Equal before Truth,' " KM, June 1, 1966, SCMP, no. 3730 [July 1, 1966], p. 1). " 'Everybody is equal before the truth' is from beginning to end a bourgeois slogan which is hypocritical in every respect. Between antagonistic classes, there is basically no equality to speak of" (In "Long Live the Great Revolution of the Proletariat," p. 9).

40. Mao wrote: "Where do correct ideas come from? Do they drop from the skies? No. Are they innate in the mind? No. They come from social practice, and from it alone; they come from three kinds of social practice, the struggle for production, the class struggle and scientific experiment. It is man's social being that determines his thinking. Once the correct ideas characteristic of the advanced class are grasped by the masses, these ideas turn into a material force

which changes society and changes the world. . . . At first knowledge is perceptual. The leap to conceptual knowledge, i.e., to ideas, occurs when sufficient perceptual knowledge is accumulated. This is one process in cognition. It is the first stage in the whole process of cognition, the stage leading from objective matter to subjective consciousness, from existence to ideas. Whether or not one's consciousness or ideas (including theories, policies, plans or measures) do correctly reflect the laws of the objective external world is not yet proved at this stage, in which it is not yet possible to ascertain whether they are correct or not. Then comes the second stage in the process of cognition, the stage leading from consciousness back to matter, from ideas back to existence, in which the knowledge gained in the first stage is applied in social practice to ascertain whether the theories, policies, plans or measures meet with the anticipated success. Generally speaking, those that succeed are correct and those that fail are incorrect, and this is especially true of man's struggle with nature" (Mao Zedong, "Where Do Correct Ideas Come From?" in *FEP*, pp. 134–35).

41. Mao wrote: "In social struggle, the forces representing the advanced class sometimes suffer defeat not because their ideas are incorrect but because, in the balance of forces engaged in struggle, they are not as powerful for the time being as the forces of reaction; they are therefore temporarily defeated, but they are bound to triumph sooner or later. Man's knowledge makes another leap through the test of practice. This leap is more important than the previous one. For it is this leap alone that can prove the correctness or incorrectness of the first leap, i.e., of the ideas, theories, policies, plans or measures formulated in the course of reflecting the objective external world. There is no other way of testing truth. Furthermore, the one and only purpose of the proletariat in knowing the world is to change it. Often, a correct idea can be arrived at only after many repetitions of the process leading from matter to consciousness and then back to matter, that is, leading from practice to knowledge and then back to practice. Such is the Marxist theory of knowledge, the dialectical materialist theory of knowledge" (FEP, pp. 135–36).

42. Chang Yu-lou, "Marxist Method of Class Analysis and Historical Research," PD, June 18, 1963, SCMP, no. 3018 (July 15, 1963), p. 5.

STRUGGLE AND HOPE

Is life nothing but struggle? Our discussion has shown that in Mao's view life is much more than struggle. The Maoist ethic emphasizes love and concern among the people, personal development and growth, and projects a vision of a future in which a fuller life will be shared by all. Struggle is combined with a deep, pervasive hope and optimism about the future of humanity.

Struggle and hope in the Maoist world view form part of a set of beliefs or ethical assumptions that have been referred to at various points in the discussion. I will review these beliefs here and then go on to indicate the significance of my encounter with Mao's world view for my own life and thought, which I believe is also of significance for others.

Maoist Beliefs

Three basic Maoist beliefs were discussed in the first chapter: contradiction, justice, and destiny. The understanding that struggle and contradiction pervade all natural and human phenomena seems to be beyond scientific or logical proof. It

143

represents an approach to the world that may be useful for analysis, but is more a hypothesis than an observable fact. Belief in the omnipresence of contradiction in the social realm in terms of class struggle and permanent revolution is, nevertheless, one of the mainsprings of Mao's ethical thought.

Mao often said that the people's struggle will triumph against oppression because their cause is just. This belief in the ultimate victory of justice seems even more remote from scientific proof. One might argue that in human history injustice has a higher score. The lack of a scientific proof, however, does not make belief in the ultimate triumph of justice any less powerful as an ethical force.

Hope, or a vision of the future, is also a core ethical belief in Mao's philosophy. He had a sense of human destiny beyond exploitation and oppression. It is not possible to live now as if this future classless society were already achieved. On the other hand, it is considered incorrect to live and work in a way that ignores this future goal or neglects movement toward it.[1] There is movement in human history, according to Mao, in which the ultimate advantage is on the side of the just cause of the people and which progresses toward the goal of a more human future.

These beliefs of Mao are paradoxical. How can revolution be permanent if it is moving toward a goal? Either it will achieve its goal, and therefore is not permanent, or it will not reach its goal and therefore is directionless or futile. Without the goal, revolutionary movement becomes meaningless. Achievement of the goal, however, would mean the end of life and history and movement. The affirmation both of hope and permanent struggle describes human reality better than would the denial of either of these two elements. This paradox gives Mao's ethic its dynamic dimension.

Another aspect of Mao's thought that falls into the category of belief is his understanding of good and evil. Proletarian, for Mao, means the good. If a proletarian acts in a selfish manner it is because of bourgeois corruption. Bourgeois is identified with the bad. These terms take on the role of ethical symbolism. It is assumed that workers and peasants are inclined toward a higher ethical standard than others in society. The problem of the source of evil is explained (by inference) both in terms of the corruption that comes in history because of the rise of classes in society and in terms of the unending development of new contradictions in all social phenomena.

Mao also believes in what might be called "human spirituality." The human is put in a primary place. In war, says Mao, it is not weapons but people that make the final difference. Human will and consciousness are able to change the world. For this reason continued thought struggle (the struggle of the human soul or self-revolution) is of central importance. While Mao would deny any religious or "transcendent" dimension, there is in his writings a groping after meaning that goes beyond the strictly mundane. The emphasis on thought, spirit, soul, although not religious in the traditional sense, suggests a depth of meaning in life that surpasses the flat secularism of a mechanical or technological approach to the world. Mao has a sense of historical movement "independent of the human will." The movement toward justice, based on a hope for a future without exploitation, requires human effort, but follows historical principles that cannot simply be overturned by the will of the oppressors. There is in Mao a kind of human or secular spirituality, a revolutionary humanism, that defies any simple categorization in traditional terms.

Mao has taken Marxism, a philosophy that developed in the soil of the Judeo-Christian-humanist traditions of Europe, and indigenized it for China. Maoism is one example of Third World Marxism, a total phenomenon that deserves greater attention. A system of thought has been developed in China that combines West and East. For a Westerner to encounter Maoism is to encounter something both familiar and strange. This Easternized Western thought and action appears as a rich and fruitful contribution to the quest for justice and truth.

Marxism developed in the context of European thought but made a radical critique of the religion and liberalism of nineteenth-century Europe. The Maoist critique of liberal humanism and religion follows Marx and develops the critique on the basis of China's own experience. Countries that were the victims of Western imperialism obviously see imperialism in very graphic terms. Western religion and liberal humanism were at home, by and large, with the powers of imperialism and were identified in the minds of the Chinese with enemy powers.

One encounters in Mao's thought both a philosophy that has echoes of the Judeo-Christian and liberal traditions that pervade the West, and a radical rejection of these traditions. Mao's passion for justice, sense of history, and vision of the future are not at all foreign to the moral and religious traditions of the West. The difference comes in Mao's steady focus on the central issue of class struggle.

A deep sense of justice underlies Marx's analysis of the suffering and struggle of the proletariat. Mao's China experienced directly the imperial power of Western capitalism. The very system that victimized China also proclaimed liberal values such as equality and liberty. From Marx and from experience, the issue of class struggle was clearly focused for Mao and the Chinese revolutionaries. The belief in class struggle is like a knife the Chinese use to cut through the hypocrisy of the professed values of the West. Judeo-Christian passion for justice and sense of history were turned against the imperial powers that kept these values in name while inflicting upon the Chinese all kinds of injustices.

It is necessary to distinguish between the *content* of certain values and their *function*. Liberty, equality, and love are rejected by Mao because they became slogans that functioned to disguise reality. While proclaiming these values Western powers are able, at the same time, to ignore the vast economic inequalities that make a mockery of liberty, equality, and love. Mao will not let us in the West talk glibly about love and equality while we are living off the blood and sweat of the world's poor. The radical content of "liberty, equality, fraternity" is reaffirmed in Mao's revolutionary humanism in terms of liberation, the mass line, and serving the people. In the revolutionary struggle ethic, however, class struggle is still kept central, giving a dynamism and an integrity to Mao's ethic that radically transforms the old values.

In the Maoist ethic, struggle continues because new growth and new progress are always possible. Even in a socialist society, where the injustices and the indignities of economic disparity have been mitigated, class struggle continues. Self-revolutionization continues also, that is, class struggle in the thought or mind. Revolution and self-revolution are permanent processes. Contradictions, it is said, will continue for ten thousand years, even after the extinction of the sun. A classless society can be achieved in human history, but the Chinese give a new twist to this. Even in classless society revolutionary struggle will continue. There will still be contradictions between the advanced and the backward. The classless society is not the culmination of history but only one more stage. There will be new worlds to conquer.

The Maoist ethic, then, has both a historical and a suprahistorical dimension. To oversimplify, on the strictly historical level evil arose because of the rise of classes; exploitative tendencies have been learned from generation to generation and long, difficult processes of education will be needed to overcome them; but through revolution and re-education under the dictatorship of the proletariat it will be possible to overcome the evils of exploitation and build a classless society. On the suprahistorical level, all phenomena are characterized by contradiction; in history there are and always will be contradiction and struggle; class struggle is one instance of the contradictions that pervade everything; after classes have been eliminated and a classless society established there will still be contradictions and struggle and revolution; and in the soul or mind of every person there will always be a struggle between good and evil, selfishness and selflessness, individual and community interests.

The Maoist ethic, it can be said, functions on the purely historical plane but also includes a grand vision of the world and life that is suprahistorical. Mao is not just a visionary, however, talking on the grand scale of eternal contradiction. Mao is a revolutionary, and it is possible to see his thought and ethic in terms of the revolutionary changes in China. It is not Mao's thought, but the reality of Chinese society that makes the initial impact on the outside observer, a society that for all its faults has opened new patterns of human interrelations. It is because of the reality of what is already happening in China that one is led to investigate the broader dimension of Mao's vision.

Encounter with Mao's Thought

I approach Mao's thought as an outsider, coming from another tradition, another culture. What I experience can be described as a personal encounter, not a confrontation. Mao's thought is something different, something other, but it represents a force for transformation in Chinese society that draws me, as an observer, into creative involvement.

Mao's ethic, as I have said, is a Chinese indigenization of the Western philosophy of Marx and strikes us as something both familiar and strange. It cannot be taken over in the West without adaptation, any more than Marxism could be taken over in China without adaptation. Mao's ethic is an ethic for China. The experience of Chinese society, the human progress that has resulted from the Chinese revolution, and the thought of Mao with all its spiritual dimensions make this ethic one that cannot be ignored by people anywhere who are concerned about justice and revolution and human progress. The world's encounter with Mao's ethic has only just begun.

In this encounter with Mao's thought I find myself driven back to the roots of concern for justice in my Western heritage and also driven forward to a deeper understanding of the economic inequalities and victimization that my Western heritage has been able to disguise. The centrality of class struggle in Mao's thought and action comes as a challenge to my ethics. The question of class struggle is a question of where I stand, whom I serve, what I practice. It is not possible for me simply to believe in love and justice and to go on in relative comfort while other people suffer in unloving and unjust situations that result from the plunder and exploitation perpetrated by my own nation and society. My ethical response to the world cannot be only the espousal of certain causes, but must also include a critique of the class structures in which I live and move and have my social being. If such a critique is to have any integrity, it must move me toward self-revolutionization and toward social revolution.

This encounter with Mao's thought leads me to a new ethical language and a new understanding of world history and self. By new language I mean terms such as human or secular spirituality and the struggle of the soul in self-revolution. Mao was a Marxist revolutionary, an atheist, a political and military leader. He spoke, however, in terms of human destiny, the human spirit, and deep personal transformation. This secular spirituality has no direct counterpart in my own life and culture. Like many others, however, I am seeking a new understanding that moves beyond old patterns of thought, while preserving a concern which goes deeper than a mere technological or mechanical view of human life. Mao combines secular spirituality with a consistent grounding in politics, production, social revolution, and everyday human relations.

This combining of human spirituality with the realities of life and struggle makes Mao's view challenging and lends a new dimension to my understanding of world history. History is seen as the ceaseless struggle of contending classes. This view does not mean that I espouse conflict or oppose peace and harmony. It means that justice and peace can be achieved only through struggle, even though that struggle may sometimes be violent. Liberal rhetoric must be cut away to see realistically the interests represented by specific policies and practices.

As examples, United States aid programs are lauded for their humanitarian value when, in fact, they give military support to oppressive regimes (as in the Philippines and South Korea) in order to preserve U.S. economic interests. Programs to combat poverty in the United States have often only provided good salaries to those administering the programs without dealing with the basic causes of poverty, which can be solved only by a struggle to change power relations. Universities receive a significant proportion of our society's resources, but function largely to perpetuate class differences. Overemphasis on individual freedom, without community responsibility and discipline, also contributes to the maintenance of economic class disparities. Our systems of education and health care do not give primary place to industrial and farm workers, but favor those of position and wealth. Too many of the resources of our society are controlled by a minority for selfish use, rather than by the people for community use. Historical processes need to be analyzed in terms of how persons and groups seek to maintain or to combat this class oppression.

Encounter with Mao's thought also leads to a new understanding of self. It may be easy for me to assume a false academic objectivity when looking at the issues of economic oppression. The Maoist approach, by relating these issues to the ethical struggle that goes on in the thought or soul, forces me to ask myself which class interests are reflected in my life and action.

"What is my class stand?" "Whom do I serve?"—these are very discomforting ethical questions. I must ask myself the degree to which selfish aims control my decisions—the desire to establish myself, to have certain comforts, to gain recognition or other rewards.

In Mao's China, these moral criteria play an active role. The standards by which people judge themselves are very demanding. Is one willing to identify with the life and situation of the ordinary workers? Is one willing to do the dirty and difficult jobs, without seeking special rewards? Does one take a position of responsibility as an opportunity for personal gain or as an opportunity to serve the people better?

The call to self-sacrifice is not exclusively Maoist, nor does this spirit characterize everyone in China. A new dimension is added in the Maoist system, however, since personal sacrifice is part of a total social system that gives primary place to community rather than personal achievement. In other systems self-sacrifice on the part of ordinary people may simply lead to their being further exploited by those in power. In China the struggle against selfishness and inequality pervades the whole society from top to bottom. There are variations and imperfections, of course, but by and large the Chinese system stands as a challenge to the selfishness at the heart of Western capitalism and revisionism.

Self-sacrifice in the West is frequently expressed as a religious value, abstracted from social realities. It is often seen as an individual calling with no necessary social impact. In Mao's ethic the struggle against selfishness is integrally related to the struggle against class structures of exploitation. This is why it is called thought struggle or self-revolution. Self-revolution and social revolution are part of one process.

The question raised in my encounter with Mao's thought, of my class stand or whom I serve, is not simply a personal internal matter that I can deal with in some sort of monastic seclusion. My thought struggle can take place realistically only in the midst of society and in revolutionary struggle against the enemies of the people who live by oppression and exploitation.

The Marxist concept of class struggle has a long history and is not new with Mao. China, however, has developed the struggle ethic in a new and compelling way. Egalitarian plain living and hard struggle are practiced to a degree not previously witnessed in any large society. A style of life has been developed that provides cultural dignity, political awareness, and community involvement for the broad masses of the people. Productive labor, health care, education, women's liberation, care for the aged and infirm, a healthy environment, a sense of purpose are present in Chinese society in a way that gives a new hope for humanity. This hope remains in spite of the shortcomings and imperfections that continue in China's policy and practice. The human development witnessed in China makes the struggle ethic upon which it is based an approach to life that I cannot easily put aside.

Life, in Mao's view, is more than struggle, but it is never less than struggle. Each person is constantly called on to enter the struggle, to choose a class stand, to fight selfishness, to serve the people. Social transformation, self-revolution, the need for frugality and struggle are never-ending. Revolution is permanent, but it moves toward fulfillment. That fulfillment stands only at the end of human history, for without contradiction and struggle life itself would end.

Mao's struggle ethic is compelling to me because it rings true. This ethic has been the basis of exciting human development within China and it provides a useful tool for analyzing social conflict in other contexts. I also find that the struggle ethic relates intimately to my personal moral decisions. Neutrality in social struggle is not an option. I either go counter to the revolutionary movement of history or I contribute my energies to the struggle for human justice. This imperative to choose, to act, to identify with the oppressed, and to engage in self-criticism goes to the depths of my thought and life. To study Mao and the Chinese revolution is not simply an academic exercise; it is a deeply personal encounter.

NOTE

1. Hsu Li-ch'un, "Have We Already Reached the Stage of Communism," RF 12 (November 16, 1958), ECMM, no. 156 (January 26, 1959), p. 5.

IN THE AUTUMN COLD

Mao's death came five decades after he penned the lines of poetry quoted in the first chapter (p. 19). Many people in China and beyond who were touched by his life and work cannot but feel "alone in the autumn cold."

These fifty years witnessed the triumph of the revolution and the transformation of the land of China. China's experience had an impact throughout Asia, Africa, and Latin America. At Mao's death there was an outpouring of tribute from all corners of the world. The obituary in the Toronto *Star,* by Jerome Ch'en, summed up the thoughts of many when it heralded Mao as a "fierce rebel with a love for humanity."

The death of Mao does not mean the end of the Mao era, but perhaps only its beginning. The love and struggle that have been discerned in Mao's philosophy and action will continue, because they are a basic component in human history.

People wonder what China will do without Mao. A "de-Maoization" in China, like the de-Stalinization that occurred in Russia, is highly improbable. There may be a period of uncertainty. There may be a period of "Maoist scholasticism," literal interpretation of Mao's philosophy without the daring to engage in consequent action. I am sanguine enough, however, to think that China will get on with the revolution.

Why do we wonder how China will get along without Mao? Is it a tendency to look to Mao and the Chinese revolution for a vicarious revolutionary experience? Do we expect China to carry the torch for the rest of us?

The death of Mao should lead us to ask not what China will do without Mao, but what we will do about Mao and all that he stood for—plain living, the fight against oppression, the struggle to build a society of justice and unity.

GLOSSARY OF CHINESE NAMES AND TERMS

In the Glossary below, personal and place names using the new romanization are followed by traditional romanizations in parentheses. When the traditional romanization is retained this is noted. The new romanization does not use hyphens in personal names.

The following variations are the most significant for the reader:

New Romanization	Old Romanization
b	p
c	ts'
ch	ch'
d	t
g	k
j	ch
k	k'
p	p'
q	ch'
r	j
t	t'
x	hs,s
z	ts
zh	ch

bo ai

博爱

Broad or universal love.

bugandang

不敢当

"I would not dare consider it so."
A polite denial of a compliment.

Chen Yunggui
(Ch'en Yung-kwei)

陈永贵

Peasant leader, rose to fame and
national position for turning
Dazhai into a model commune.

Chiang Kai-shek

蒋介石

Former leader of Chinese
Nationalist Party (traditional
spelling retained).

Ch'ing *see* Qing

清

Chou En-lai
see Zhou Enlai

周恩来

Dazhai (Tachai)

大寨

Model commune in Shanxi Province.

dousi pixiu

斗私批修

Fight self and repudiate revisionism.

duikangxing

对抗性

Antagonistic. A contradiction
between people and enemy is
antagonistic.

duli sikao

独立思考

Independence of thought.

fanshen

翻身

To turn over. A deep change of attitude, as from servitude to self-respect.

ganbu

干部

Cadre; a functionary or teacher not directly engaged in productive physical labor.

hong (hung)

红

Red; carries positive moral and political connotations.

Hong Kong

香港

A city in southern Guangdong Province, under British administration since the 1840 Opium War (traditional spelling retained).

Hunan

湖南

A province in central China (same spelling in both romanizations).

Jiangxi (Kiangsi)

江西

A province in central China.

jianku fendou

艰苦奋斗

Plain living and hard struggle.

jieji chushen

阶级出身

Class status or class origin.

jieji lichang

阶级立场

Class stand.

Jinggang Shan
(Chingkangshan)

井冈山

Mountain area in Jiangxi Province where Mao established an early stronghold.

jingshenshang

精神上

Spiritual, having to do with mind or spirit; moral, in the sense of moral support.

Lei Feng

雷锋

A soldier hero of the early 1960s (same spelling in both romanizations).

Lin Biao
(Lin Piao)

林彪

One-time defense minister, leader of the Cultural Revolution, once considered heir apparent to Mao; reported to have died in a plane crash in 1971 after allegedly attempting to assassinate Mao.

Liu Shaoqi
(Liu Shao-ch'i)

刘少奇

Former head of state, disgraced in the Cultural Revolution.

Lu Xun (Lu Hsun)

鲁迅

Radical author of the 1920s.

Mao Zedong
(Mao Tse-tung)

毛泽东

Late chairman of the Chinese Communist Party.

Ming 明	Ruling dynasty, A.D. 1368–1644 (same spelling as both romanizations).
Peking 北京	Capital city of the People's Republic of China (traditional spelling retained).
Qing (Ch'ing) 清	Last imperial dynasty, ended in 1911.
Shanghai 上海	Port on the Yangtze estuary, China's largest city (same spelling in both romanizations).
Shanxi (Shansi) 山西	Province in North-central China.
si 私	Self, selfish; ego, egoism; private, as opposed to community.
sixiang gaizao 思想改造	Thought reform, ideological remolding.
Sun Yat-sen 孙中山（逸仙）	Leader of the 1911 revolution in China (traditional spelling retained).
Suzhou (Soochow) 苏州	City in Jiangsu Province.
Taiwan 台湾	Island province of China (same spelling in both romanizations).

tu
土

Native, indigenous; literally "land" or "of the land."

Wang Yangming
王阳明

Neo-Confucian scholar of the Ming dynasty (same spelling in both romanizations).

xiuzhengzhuyi
修正主义

Revisionism.

Yanan (Yenan)
延安

Revolutionary base area of Mao's forces during the Japan war and after.

yang
洋

Foreign; literally "sea" or "from overseas."

Yao Wenyuan
姚文元

Shanghai literary critic and theoretician; leader of the Cultural Revolution (same spelling in both romanizations).

Zhou Enlai
(Chou En-lai)
周恩来

Late premier of China; lifelong leader of the revolution.

Zhou Zuoren
(Chou Tso-ren)
周作人

Author prominent in the 1920s and 1930s, considered by Mao to be a traitor.

zi
自

Self; not necessarily connoting selfish, except in combination with *si*.

zichan jieji

资产阶级

Bourgeois; capitalist class.

zili gengsheng

自力更生

Self-reliance.

zisi

自私

Selfish.

ziwo geming

自我革命

Self-revolution, self-revolution-ization.

ABBREVIATIONS USED IN NOTES

CB   *Current Background,* U.S. Consulate, Hong Kong. Translations from Chinese journals and newspapers, selected according to topical interest.

CY   *China Youth,* Peking. A journal for young people, discontinued in 1966 at the time of the Cultural Revolution.

CYN   *China Youth Newspaper,* Peking. A newspaper for young people which also stopped publication in 1966.

ECMM   *Excerpts from China Mainland Magazines,* U.S. Consulate, Hong Kong. Translations from Chinese journals. The name of the journal was altered twice, but the numbering system continued without interruption.
See SCMM and SPRCM below.

FEP   Mao Tse-tung, *Four Essays in Philosophy,* Peking: Foreign Languages Press, 1966.

KM   *Kwang Ming Jih-pao (Guangming Ribao),* Peking. An important daily newspaper.

PD   *People's Daily,* Peking. China's leading national newspaper.

RF   *Red Flag,* Peking. Theoretical journal of the Chinese Communist Party.

SCMM   *Survey of Chinese Mainland Magazines.* Succeeded ECMM, preceded SPRCM.

SCMP   *Survey of Chinese Mainland Press,* U.S. Consulate, Hong Kong. Translations of articles from Chinese daily newspapers. The name of the journal was altered once, but the numbering system continued without interruption. *See* SPRCP.

SPRCM   *Survey of People's Republic of China Magazines.* Succeeded ECMM and SCMM.

SPRCP   *Survey of People's Republic of China Press.* Succeeded SCMP.

SW   Mao Tse-tung, *Selected Works of Mao Tse-tung,* 4 vols., Peking: Foreign Languages Press, vol. 4, 1961; vols. 1–3, 1965.

INDEX

166   *Index*